PREFACE

Here is a complete set of revision notes to aid your preparation for all current CSE, 'O' level and 16+ examinations in mathematics. Not all the topics included here will be examined by some examination boards, so check the syllabus requirements of your course and select from the comprehensive contents list which is provided for your use. Plan your revision carefully, and give yourself plenty of time to cover all aspects of the syllabus thoroughly. Hopefully these revision cards will bring you success.

Acknowledgements

My thanks go to Peter Noon, deputy-head of the mathematics department at Stopsley High School, Luton, for carefully checking the original typescript, and for providing me with some useful additional material and suggestions. I am also grateful to David Symes for his help in preparing the contents for publication.

E. Wakeling
1984

GW00420309

CONTENTS

1 SETS

Definitions and symbols
1 A set is a collection of items.
2 The items in a set are called its **elements**.
3 The elements of a set may be listed:
$$V = \{a, e, i, o, u\}$$
or described:
$$V = \{\text{the vowels of the alphabet}\}$$
4 The complete set of all possible elements is called the **universal set**, $\mathscr{E}$. In this case $\mathscr{E} = \{\text{the letters of the alphabet}\} = \{a, b, c, d \ldots\}$.
5 $u \in V$ means that the letter u is in the set V.
6 $f \notin V$ means that the letter f is *not* in the set V.
7 The **number of elements** in set V is five:
$$n(V) = 5$$
8 Some special sets of number:
   ⋆ $N = \{\text{natural numbers}\} = \{1, 2, 3, 4 \ldots\}$
   ⋆ $Z = \{\text{integers}\} = \{\ldots -3, -2, -1, 0, 1, 2, 3 \ldots\}$
   These sets have an infinite number of elements.
9 The elements in a set need not be ordered:
$$V = \{a, e, i, o, u,\} = \{e, u, i, a, o\} = \{u, a, o, e, i\}$$
10 The elements in a set are not repeated:
$$T = \{\text{the letters in the word 'toffee'}\} = \{t, o, f, e\}$$

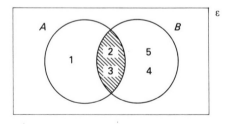

Fig. 1.1 *Intersection* $A \cap B$

8

Operations

1 If $A = \{1, 2, 3\}$ and $B = \{2, 3, 4, 5\}$, then the **intersection** of these two sets is $A \cap B = \{2, 3\}$. This is shown by the shaded region in the Venn diagram in Fig. 1.1.

2 The **union** of these sets is $A \cup B = \{1, 2, 3, 4, 5\}$. This is shown by the shaded region in Fig. 1.2.

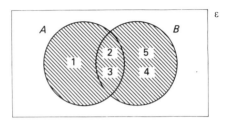

Fig. 1.2 *Union* $A \cup B$

3 If $C = \{7, 8\}$, then $A \cap C = \{\}$, called the **empty set**, written as $\emptyset$. These sets are said to be disjoint. This is shown in Fig. 1.3.

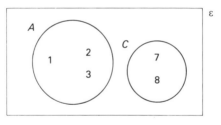

Fig. 1.3. $A \cap C = \emptyset$

4 If $D = \{2, 5\}$, then the elements of set D are contained within set B. We say that D is a **subset** of B and write $D \subset B$. This is shown in Fig. 1.4.

9

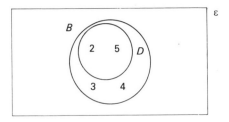

Fig. 1.4 $D \subset B$

5 If the universal set is
$$\mathscr{E} = \{n : 1 \leqslant n \leqslant 10, n \in Z\}$$
it means that the set contains numbers n such that n lies between 1 and 10 inclusively, and n is from the set of integers (i.e. a whole number):
$$\mathscr{E} = \{1, 2, 3, 4, 5, 6, 7, 8, 9, 10\}$$

6 The elements *not* in set A, but in the universal set $\mathscr{E}$, are $\{4, 5, 6, 7, 8, 9, 10\}$. This is called the **complement** of set A and is written as A'. The complement of set A is shaded in Fig. 1.5.

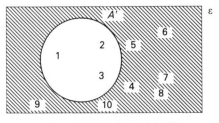

Fig. 1.5 $A \cup A' = \mathscr{E}$; $A \cap A' = \varnothing$

Regions of a Venn diagram
The four regions of a Venn diagram, showing the intersection of

two subsets P and Q of the universal set $\mathscr{E}$, are labelled a, b, c, d (see Fig. 1.6.).

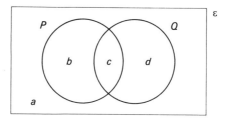

Fig. 1.6

Set	Region	Set	Region
P	b and c	$P\cup Q$	b, c and d
P'	a and d	$P'\cap Q$	d
Q	c and d	$P\cap Q'$	b
Q'	a and b	$P'\cap Q'$	a
$P\cap Q$	c	$P'\cup Q'$	a, b and d

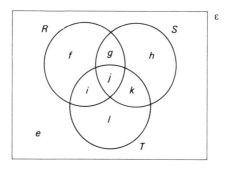

Fig. 1.7

11

By shading the appropriate regions of a Venn diagram it can be shown that:
1 $(A \cup B)'=A' \cap B'$
2 $(A \cap B)'=A' \cup B'$
These are **De Morgan's laws**.

The eight regions of a Venn diagram, showing the intersection of three subsets R, S and T of the universal set $\mathscr{E}$, are labelled e, f, g, h, i, j, k, l (see Fig. 1.7).

Set	Region	Set	Region
R	f, g, i, j	$R \cap S' \cap T'$	f
S	g, h, j, k	$R' \cap S \cap T'$	h
T	i, j, k, l	$R' \cap S' \cap T$	l
$R \cap S \cap T$	j	$R \cap S \cap T'$	g
$R \cap S$	g, j	$R' \cap S \cap T$	k
$S \cap T$	j, k	$R \cap S' \cap T$	i
$R \cap T$	i, j	$R' \cap S' \cap T'$	e

By shading the appropriate regions of a Venn diagram it can be show that:
1 $R \cup (S \cup T)=(R \cup S) \cup T$ (**associative law**)
2 $R \cap (S \cap T)=(R \cap S) \cap T$ (**associative law**)
3 $R \cap (S \cup T)=(R \cap S) \cup (R \cap T)$ (**distributive law**)
4 $R \cup (S \cap T)=(R \cup S) \cap (R \cup T)$ (**distributive law**)

Coordinate sets
1 $G=\{(x, y):y=2x, 0<x<4, x \in Z\}$
  ⋆ This is a set of coordinate points, (x, y).
  ⋆ The points lie on the straight line with equation $y=2x$.
  ⋆ The values of x are integral and range between 0 and 4 exclusively (see Fig. 1.8).

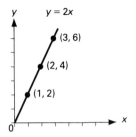

Fig. 1.8

* So $G = \{(1, 2), (2, 4), (3, 6)\}$
2 $H = \{(x, y):x+y<5, x\in N, y\in N\}$
   * This is also a set of coordinate points, (x, y).
   * The points lie in the region bounded by the x axis, the y axis (positive integers) and the line with equation $x+y=5$ (see Fig. 1.9).

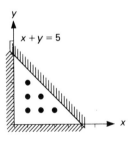

Fig. 1.9

★ So $H = \{(1, 1), (1, 2), (1, 3), (2, 1), (2, 2), (3, 1)\}$.

Set problems

A Venn diagram is used in these cases to show the **number of elements** in a particular region.

Example: In a class of 30 pupils, 20 like milk and 24 like lemonade. There are 2 pupils who like neither drink. How many pupils like both drinks?

2 pupils like neither drink, so 28 like at least one of the drinks. $(20 + 24) - 28 = 16$ like both drinks (see Fig. 1.10).

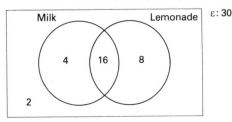

Fig. 1.10

14

2 NUMBER

Definitions

1 **Natural** or counting numbers are positive whole numbers:
   $$N = \{1, 2, 3, 4 \ldots\}$$

2 **Integers** are positive and negative whole numbers and zero:
   $$Z = \{\ldots {}^-3, {}^-2, {}^-1, 0, {}^+1, {}^+2, {}^+3 \ldots\}$$

3 **Rational numbers** are all numbers, positive and negative, which can be expressed as a fraction (or ratio), $\frac{p}{q}$, where p and q are integers $(q \neq 0)$:
   $$\left\{-8, -\tfrac{1}{2}, 0, \tfrac{1}{3}, \tfrac{7}{8}, 1, 1\tfrac{3}{4}, 3\tfrac{2}{3}\right\}$$
   The above set is a selection of rational numbers; the complete set is called **Q**.

4 **Irrational numbers** are positive and negative numbers which are non-rational numbers such as:
   $$\pi = 3.1415927 \ldots \text{ and } \sqrt{2} = 1.4142136 \ldots$$

5 **Real numbers** are all numbers, rational and irrational. The arrangement of all real numbers is shown in the Venn diagram in Fig. 2.1.

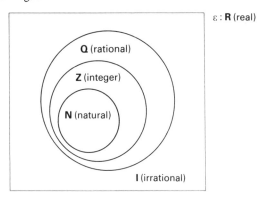

Fig. 2.1 *Arrangement of all real numbers*

15

Properties of natural numbers

1 The **factors** of a natural number are other natural numbers which divide exactly into the number.

$A = \{\text{factors of } 15\} = \{1, 3, 5, 15\}$

2 **Prime** numbers have only *two* factors, themselves and 1.

$P = \{\text{prime numbers}\} = \{2, 3, 5, 7, 11 \ldots\}$

Note that 1 is not a prime number (only one factor) but 2 is a prime number (the only even prime).

3 The **multiples** of a number are found by multiplying the number by each natural number in turn, producing a sequence of multiples often called the times-table of the number.

$M = \{\text{multiples of } 7\} = \{7, 14, 21, 28, 35 \ldots\}$

4 The **highest common factor** (HCF) of two or more numbers is the largest number which will divide exactly into them without remainder. The HCF of 12 and 18 is 6.

5 The **lowest common multiple** (LCM) of two or more numbers is the smallest number which is exactly divisible by them. The LCM of 3, 4 and 6 is 12.

6 **Prime factors** are factors of a number which are also prime numbers. The prime factors of 350 are 2, 5 and 7.

7 The number 350 may be written as a **product of primes**:

$350 = 2 \times 5 \times 5 \times 7$
$350 = 2 \times 5^2 \times 7$

8 Any natural number which is not a prime number is a **rectangular number**.

$R = \{\text{rectangular numbers}\} = \{1, 4, 6, 8, 9, 10 \ldots\}$

9 A subset of the rectangular numbers is the set of **square numbers**. Square numbers are the product of two equal natural numbers, e.g. 1×1, 2×2, 3×3 ... (see Fig. 2.2). They are natural numbers with an odd number of factors.

Fig. 2.2 *Square numbers*

$S = \{\text{square numbers}\} = \{1, 4, 9, 16, 25 \ldots\}$

Number sequences

A sequence is a set of numbers which follows a pattern or rule. Here are some examples of well-known sequences listed as infinite sets.

1 **Odd numbers** $= \{1, 3, 5, 7, 9, 11 \ldots\}$
2 **Even numbers** $= \{2, 4, 6, 8, 10, 12 \ldots\}$
3 **Triangular numbers** $= \{1, 3, 6, 10, 15 \ldots\}$ (see Fig. 2.3).

Fig. 2.3 *Triangular numbers*

Number operations

Let b, r and w be any three real numbers.

Addition

1 **Commutative law:** $b + r = r + b$
2 **Associative law:** $(b + r) + w = b + (r + w)$
3 Zero is the **identity** element for addition, since:
   $b + 0 = b$
4 The **additive inverse** of b is $-b$, since:
   $b + (-b) = 0$ (the identity)

Multiplication

1 **Commutative law:** $b \times r = r \times b$
2 **Associative law:** $(b \times r) \times w = b \times (r \times w)$
3 One is the **identity** element for multiplication, since:
   $b \times 1 = b$
4 The **multiplicative inverse** of b is $\frac{1}{b}$, since:

$$b \times \frac{1}{b} = 1 \text{ (the identity)}$$

Note: a number combined with its inverse gives the identity for that operation.

Distribution

This is multiplication over addition:

$$b(r+w) = br + bw$$

Note: br means b multiplied by r.

Order of operations

Number operations follow this order of priority.

1 Brackets.
2 Powers.
3 Multiplication; division.
4 Addition; subtraction.

$$6 + 3(7-2)^2 = 6 + 3 \times 5^2 = 6 + 3 \times 25 = 6 + 75 = 81$$

Group structure

1 **Closure:** a set of elements is said to be closed under an operation if combining the elements by that operation always gives a member of the same set.
2 A **group** is a set of elements which are combined by an operation such that:
   ★ there is an identity element in the set:
   ★ each element has a unique inverse in the set;
   ★ the set is closed under the operation;
   ★ the associative law for the operation holds.

Directed number

1 **Positive numbers** are signed like this: $^+3$.
2 **Negative numbers** are signed like this: $^-3$.
3 These examples will illustrate the **addition** of directed numbers:

$$^+3 + {^+4} = {^+7} \qquad\qquad ^-3 + {^+4} = {^+1}$$
$$^+3 + {^-4} = {^-1} \qquad\qquad ^-3 + {^-4} = {^-7}$$

4 These examples will illustrate the **subtraction** of directed numbers:

$$^+3-^+4=^-1 \qquad\qquad ^-3-^+4=^-7$$
$$^+3-^-4=^+7 \qquad\qquad ^-3-^-4=^+1$$

5 These examples will illustrate the **multiplication** of directed numbers:
$$^+6\times^+2=^+12 \qquad\qquad ^-6\times^+2=^-12$$
$$^+6\times^-2=^-12 \qquad\qquad ^-6\times^-2=^+12$$

6 These examples will illustrate the **division** of directed numbers:
$$^+6\div^+2=^+3 \qquad\qquad ^-6\div^+2=^-3$$
$$^+6\div^-2=^-3 \qquad\qquad ^-6\div^-2=^+3$$

Decimals

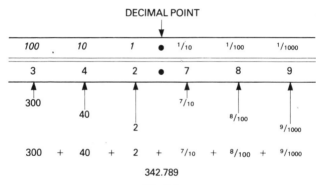

DECIMAL POINT

100	10	1	●	1/10	1/100	1/1000
3	4	2	●	7	8	9

300
40
2
$7/10$
$8/100$
$9/1000$

$$300 + 40 + 2 + 7/10 + 8/100 + 9/1000$$

342.789

Fig. 2.4

1 **Addition** (sum): keep decimal points in line. $3.72+29+0.5$ is set out like this:

```
  3.72
 29.00
  0.50+
 ─────
 33.22
```

Note: the decimal point always comes at the right-hand end of whole numbers.

19

2 Subtraction (difference): keep decimal points in line.
$4.9 - 0.153$ is set out like this:

```
 4.900
 0.153-
 ─────
 4.747
```

3 The number of digits to the right of the **decimal point** gives the **decimal places** (DP) of a decimal number.

5.127 has 3 decimal places (3 DP)

13.4 has 1 decimal place (1 DP)

4 Multiplication (product): the sum of the decimal places in the numbers to be multiplied equals the number of decimal places in the product.

5.72×1.4

(2 DP + 1 DP)

```
  572
   14×
 ─────
 5720
 2288
 ─────
 8008
```

Answer: 8.008

(3 DP)

Note: ignore the decimal point for the long multiplication.

5 Multiplication by powers of 10

$4.237 \times 10 = 42.37$

$4.237 \times 100 = 423.7$

6 Division (quotient): make the divisor into an integer by multiplying both dividend and divisor by an appropriate power of 10.

$51.96 \div 0.3$

$$\frac{\text{Dividend: } 51.96 \times 10}{\text{Divisor: } \quad 0.3 \times 10} = \frac{519.6}{3} = 3\overline{)519.6} = 173.2$$

7 Recurring decimals: dots are written above the decimal digits to show that the decimal number does not terminate but recurs.

$0.444444\ldots = 0.\dot{4}$

$0.272727\ldots = 0.\dot{2}\dot{7}$

$0.813813\ldots = 0.\dot{8}1\dot{3}$

Fractions

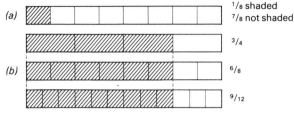

Fig. 2.5

1. A **fraction** is a way of expressing part of a whole.
   In Fig. 2.5(a), $\frac{1}{8}$ of the shape is shaded and $\frac{7}{8}$ of the shape is not shaded.

2. In Fig. 2.5(b), it will be seen that an equal amount of the shape has been shaded. This shows that there are many ways of writing the same amount as a fraction. The diagrams illustrate three **equivalent fractions**.
   $$\frac{3}{4} = \frac{6}{8} = \frac{9}{12} = \cdots$$
   Equivalent fractions are formed by multiplying the top and bottom line of the fraction by the same non-zero integer.

3. The **numerator** of $\frac{3}{4}$ is 3.

4. The **denominator** of $\frac{3}{4}$ is 4.

5. A **proper fraction** is one in which the numerator is smaller than the denominator, such as $\frac{3}{5}$.

6. An **improper fraction** is one in which the numerator is larger than the denominator, such as $\frac{5}{3}$.

7. A **mixed fraction** is the combination of an integer and a proper fraction, such as $1\frac{1}{3}$.
   Improper fractions and mixed fractions are interchangeable:
   $$\frac{22}{7} = 3\frac{1}{7}, \quad 2\frac{1}{2} = \frac{5}{2}, \quad \frac{5}{3} = 1\frac{2}{3}$$

8. If the numerator and denominator of a fraction contain numbers with an equal factor, then the fraction may be

21

cancelled down by this factor to produce an equivalent fraction.

$$\frac{14}{21} = \frac{2 \times \not{7}}{3 \times \not{7}} = \frac{2}{3} \text{ cancelling by 7}$$

Addition of fractions
Fractions need to have the same denominator for **addition**. It may be necessary to find equivalent fractions before addition can take place. The common denominator is found using the LCM of the denominators.

$$\frac{1}{4} + \frac{3}{5} = \frac{5}{20} + \frac{12}{20} = \frac{17}{20}$$

Note: the LCM of 4 and 5 is 20.

Subtraction of fractions
Fractions need to have the same denominator for subtraction.

$$\frac{7}{8} - \frac{1}{4} = \frac{7}{8} - \frac{2}{8} = \frac{5}{8}$$

Note: the LCM of 8 and 4 is 8.

Multiplication of fractions
Multiply numerators and multiply denominators, but cancel first, if possible.

$$\frac{2}{3} \times \frac{7}{10} = \frac{\not{2}^1}{3} \times \frac{7}{\not{10}_5} = \frac{7}{15}$$

Make mixed fractions into improper fractions.

$$1\frac{1}{2} \times 2\frac{2}{3} = \frac{3}{2} \times \frac{8}{3} = \frac{\not{3}^1}{\not{2}_1} \times \frac{\not{8}^4}{\not{3}_1} = \frac{4}{1} = 4$$

Division of fractions
Multiply first fraction by the multiplicative inverse of the second fraction.

$$\frac{3}{4} \div \frac{1}{2} = \frac{3}{4} \times \frac{2}{1} = \frac{3}{\not{4}_2} \times \frac{\not{2}^1}{1} = \frac{3}{2} = 1\frac{1}{2}$$

Make mixed fractions into improper fractions.

$$3\frac{1}{4} \div 2 = \frac{13}{4} \div \frac{2}{1} = \frac{13}{4} \times \frac{1}{2} = \frac{13}{8} = 1\frac{5}{8}$$

Rounding

Decimal places (DP)

1 To correct or round a number to 3 DP look at the fourth decimal place.
2 If this number is below 5, write the number as far as the third decimal place.
3 If this number is 5 or above, write the number as far as the third decimal place, but increase this third place figure by one.
4 The same procedure applies when correcting to other decimal places.

Number	Correct to 1 DP	Correct to 3 DP
4.7492	4.7	4.749
6.2835	6.3	6.284
7.9498	7.9	7.950

Significant figures (SF)

1 To correct or round a number to 3 SF look at the fourth significant figure, i.e. the fourth figure from the left ignoring the position of the decimal point and any preliminary noughts.
2 If this number is below 5, write the number as far as the third significant figure, replacing any further figures to the left of the decimal point by zero.
3 If the number is 5 or above, write the number as far as the third significant figure, but increase this third figure by one, replacing any further figures to the left of the decimal point by zero.
4 The same procedure applies when correcting to other significant figures.

23

Number	Correct to 1 SF	Correct to 3 SF
4328	4000	4330
16.44	20	16.4
0.003925	0.004	0.00393

Using a calculator

Hints for examinations

1 Do not round too soon during a calculation, otherwise you will introduce errors.
2 Do not leave answers to an inappropriate number of SF.
3 Round answers to 4 SF unless instructed to do otherwise.

Number bases

Column headings

The column headings for denary (base 10) are:

Headings: . . .	1000	100	10	1
Denary number:	3	4	7	2

$3 \times 1000 + 4 \times 100 + 7 \times 10 + 2 \times 1 = 3472$

The column headings for binary (base 2) are:

Headings: . . .	16	8	4	2	1
Binary number:	1	0	1	1	0

$1 \times 16 + 0 \times 8 + 1 \times 4 + 1 \times 2 + 0 \times 1 = 22_{10}$

The binary number 10110 is equivalent to denary number 22:

$10110_2 \equiv 22_{10}$

Note: the suffix indicates the base.

The column headings for base n are:

Headings: . . .	n^4	n^3	n^2	n^1	n^0
Base n number:	2	4	0	3	1 $(n \geqslant 5)$

$2 \times n^4 + 4 \times n^3 + 0 \times n^2 + 3 \times n^1 + 1 \times n^0 = 24031_n$

Note that $n^0 = 1$ for all number bases.

The largest digit must be at least one less than the number base. 9 is the largest digit in a denary number and 1 is the largest digit in a binary number.

Conversions

1 Into denary, e.g. change the octal number 135_8 into denary. Use the column headings of the number base.

Headings: . . .	64	8	1
Octal number:	1	3	5

$1 \times 64 + 3 \times 8 + 5 \times 1 = 93_{10}$

Therefore $135_8 \equiv 93_{10}$

2 From denary, e.g. change the denary number 27 into binary. Work from the column headings.

Headings: . . . 64 32 16 8 4 2 1

The largest required heading is 16.

Therefore $27_{10} \equiv 11011_2$ (see Fig. 2.6).

Operations

Calculations may be performed in any base. These examples in binary (base 2) and octal (base 8) will illustrate the techniques.

1 Base 2 calculations

```
   101        110        110          11
    11        11-        11×     101)1111
 1011+        ──        ────          101
 ─────         11       1100          ───
 10011                   110          101
                        ─────         101
                        10010         ───
                                        0
```

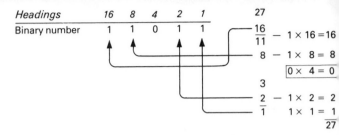

Fig. 2.6 *Conversion from denary to binary*

2 Base 8 calculations:

14	121	124	27
27	56−	14×	2)$\overline{56}$
35+	$\overline{43}$	$\overline{1240}$	4
$\overline{100}$		520	$\overline{16}$
		$\overline{1760}$	16
			$\overline{0}$

3 When base 2 (or base 8) numbers are added and multiplied, the amounts carried forward are groups of two (or groups of eight). When subtracting, groups of two (or eight) are borrowed or taken from the next column.

Modulo numbers
This is sometimes referred to as **finite** or **clock arithmetic**. Finite sets of integers are used.
1 For modulo 5 arithmetic the finite set $\{0,1,2,3,4\}$ is used.
2 For modulo n arithmetic the finite set $\{0, 1, 2, \ldots, n-1\}$ is used.

Addition
It will be seen from Fig. 2.7 that:
$1+3\equiv4 \pmod 5$ (start at 1 and move round 3 places)
and
$3+4\equiv2 \pmod 5$ (start at 3 and move round 4 places)

Note that this second example can be calculated by dividing the result by 5 and recording the remainder:

$3+4=7, 7 \div 5 = 1$ rem $2, 7 \equiv 2$ (mod 5)

Fig. 2.7 *Modulo 5 addition*

Subtraction

It will be seen from Fig. 2.8 that:

$4 - 1 \equiv 3$ (mod 5) (start at 4 and move back 1 place)

and

$1 - 2 \equiv 4$ (mod 5) (start at 1 and move back 2 places)

Note that this second example can be calculated by adding 5 to the first number.

1 (mod 5) $\equiv 6, 6 - 2 = 4$

Multiplication

The multiplication table for modulo 5 is:

x	0	1	2	3	4
0	0	0	0	0	0
1	0	1	2	3	4
2	0	2	4	1	3
3	0	3	1	4	2
4	0	4	3	2	1

From the table it will be seen that $3 \times 4 = 12 \equiv 2$ (mod 5), (start at 0 and move round 4 times 3 places in Fig. 2.7).

Division

If $3 \div 2 \equiv n$ (mod 5), then $n \times 2 \equiv 3$ (mod 5). From the multiplication table for modulo 5 given above it will be seen that

$4 \times 2 \equiv 3$ (mod 5)

Hence n is 4.

27

Fig. 2.8 *Modulo 5 subtraction*

Alternatively, add 5 (or a multiple of 5) to the first number until the division is possible without remainder;

$3 \div 2 \equiv n$ (mod 5), $8 \equiv 3$ (mod 5), $8 \div 2 = 4$, $n = 4$

Powers

1 A short way to write $3 \times 3 \times 3 \times 3$ is 3^4. This is called the **index notation**, and is read as 3 to the power 4.

2 **Squares** are power 2:
$$4^2 = 4 \times 4 = 16$$
$$8.3^2 = 8.3 \times 8.3 = 68.89$$
$$^-0.2^2 = {}^-0.2 \times {}^-0.2 = {}^+0.04$$

Squaring a number always gives a positive result.

3 **Square roots** are power $\frac{1}{2}$:
$$\sqrt{25} = +5 \text{ or } -5$$

This follows from the fact that $5 \times 5 = 25$ and $-5 \times -5 = 25$.
$$\sqrt{8.62} = \pm 2.936 \text{ (correct to 4 SF)}$$

★ All positive real numbers have two square roots.
★ There is no real square root of a negative number.
★ $\sqrt{25}$ can also be written as $25^{\frac{1}{2}}$.

4 Any number to a **zero power** is 1 (except zero itself).
$$10^0 = 1, \ 1^0 = 1, \ 27^0 = 1, \ 3^0 = 1$$

5 A **negative power** indicates a **reciprocal**.

$$3^{-1} = \frac{1}{3} \qquad 10^{-1} = \frac{1}{10} \qquad 17^{-1} = \frac{1}{17}$$
$$3^{-2} = \frac{1}{3^2} = \frac{1}{9} \qquad 10^{-3} = \frac{1}{10^3} = \frac{1}{1000}$$

6 A **fractional power** indicates a **root**.

28

$$4^{\frac{1}{2}} = \sqrt{4} = \pm 2, \quad 81^{\frac{1}{2}} = \pm 9 \text{ (square roots)}$$
$$27^{\frac{1}{3}} = \sqrt[3]{27} = 3, \quad 1000^{\frac{1}{3}} = 10 \text{ (cube roots)}$$

7 To calculate **combined powers and roots** it is usually easier to calculate the root first.

$$8^{\frac{2}{3}} = 2^2 = 4 \text{ (cube root squared)}$$
$$16^{\frac{3}{2}} = 4^3 = 64 \text{ (square root cubed)}$$

$$81^{-\frac{3}{4}} = \frac{1}{81^{\frac{3}{4}}} = \frac{1}{3^3} = \frac{1}{27} \text{ (reciprocal of fourth root cubed)}$$

Standard form (scientific notation)
This is a useful way of expressing very large and very small numbers. This notation is used by some calculators. A number is written in the form $A \times 10^n$ where n is an integer and $1 \le A < 10$.

Number	Standard form
3 700 000	3.7×10^6
12 600	1.26×10^4
0.005	5.0×10^{-3}
0.000 087 2	8.72×10^{-5}

Notice that n represents the number of places moved by the decimal point; n is positive for large numbers and negative for small numbers.

Measurement (metric)
1 These are the standard units of metric length:
   - ★ (millimetres) 10 mm = 1 cm (centimetre)
   - ★ 100 cm = 1 m (metre)
   - ★ 1000 m = 1 km (kilometre)
2 These are the standard units of metric **mass** (weight):
   - ★ (milligrams) 1000 mg = 1 g (gram)
   - ★ 1000 g = 1 kg (kilogram)
   - ★ 1000 kg = 1 tonne
3 These are the standard units of metric **capacity**:
   - ★ (millilitres) 1000 ml = 1 l (litre)
   - ★ A millilitre is 1 cubic centimetre.
   - ★ 1000 l = 1 m³

4 These are the standard units of metric **currency**:
* ★ (pence) 100p=£1 (pound)
5 **Currency conversion:**
* ★ If £1=$1.40 then an item costing £3.45 is worth:
  1.40×3.45=$4.83
* ★ If £1=SF3.05 (Swiss francs) then an item costing SF14.64 is worth:
  14.64÷3.05=£4.80

3 AREA AND VOLUME

Definitions and units of measurement
1 The length of the boundary of a shape is called the **perimeter**.
2 The amount of space contained within the boundary of a plane shape is its **area**. It is measured in squares. (This is because squares tessellate and aid the calculation of areas.)
3 The amount of space displayed by the surface of a solid shape is its **surface area**. Similarly, it is measured in squares.
4 The capacity of a solid shape is called its **volume**. It is measured in cubes.

Area of plane figures

Rectangle

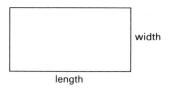

Fig. 3.1 *Rectangle*

1 Perimeter=2×length+2×width
2 Area=length×width
A rectangle of length 6 cm and width 5 cm has a perimeter of 22 cm (2×6 cm+2×5 cm), and an area of 30 cm^2 (6 cm×5 cm).

Square
A square is a special case of a rectangle. The length is equal to the width (see Fig. 3.2).
1 Perimeter=4×length
2 Area=length×length=(length)^2
A square of side 7 m has a perimeter of 28 m (4×7 m), and an

area of 49 m^2 ($7 \text{ m} \times 7 \text{ m}$).

A square of area 40 cm^2 has sides of length 6.325 cm ($\sqrt{40} = 6.325$ correct to 4 SF).

Fig. 3.2 *Square*

Triangle
1 Right-angled

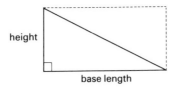

Fig. 3.3 *Right-angled triangle*

Area $= \frac{1}{2} \times$ base length $\times$ height (see Fig. 3.3).
2 Acute-angled
Area $= \frac{1}{2} \times$ base length $\times$ height (see Fig. 3.4).
3 Obtuse-angled
Area $= \frac{1}{2} \times$ base length $\times$ height (see Fig. 3.5).

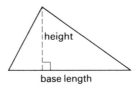

Fig. 3.4 *Acute-angled triangle*

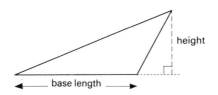

Fig. 3.5 *Obtuse-angled triangle*

Parallelogram

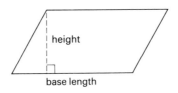

Fig. 3.6 *Parallelogram*

Area=base length×height (see Fig. 3.6).

33

Trapezium
See Fig. 3.7

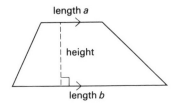

Fig. 3.7 *Trapezium; a and b are the lengths of the parallel sides*

Area $= \frac{1}{2} \times$ height $\times$ (length a + length b)

Circle
1 Circumference is the perimeter of a circle (see Fig. 3.8).

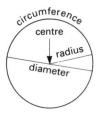

Fig. 3.8 *Circle*

Circumference $= 2 \times \pi \times$ radius $= \pi \times$ diameter. (π is a fixed constant, approximately equal to 3.142 (4 SF).)
2 Area $= \pi \times$ (radius)^2

Example: Find the circumference and area of a circle with a radius of 12 cm.

Circumference $= 2 \times 3.142 \times 12 = 12.57$ cm (4 SF).
Area $= 3.142 \times 12 \times 12 = 452.4$ cm^2 (4 SF).

3 Annulus (or ring)—see Fig. 3.9.

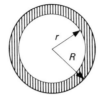

Fig. 3.9 *Annulus*

Area of shaded annulus = area of large circle (radius R)
$\qquad\qquad\qquad\qquad\qquad$ — area of small circle (radius r)
$\qquad\qquad\qquad\quad = \pi R^2 - \pi r^2$
$\qquad\qquad\qquad\quad = \pi(R-r)(R+r)$

Volume and surface area of solid shapes

Cuboid
See Fig. 3.10

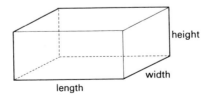

Fig. 3.10. *Cuboid*

1 Surface area=2 × length × width + 2 × width × height + 2 × length × height
2 Volume=length×width×height

Example: A cuboid of length 5 cm, width 4 cm and height 3 cm has a surface area 94 cm² $(2×5×4+2×4×3+2×5×3)$ and a volume of 60 cm³ $(5×4×3)$.

Cube

1 A cube is a special case of a cuboid with its length, width and height all equal (see Fig. 3.11).

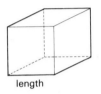

length

Fig. 3.11 *Cube*

2 Surface area=6×(length)²
3 Volume=length×length×length=(length)³
Example: A cube of side 2.65 cm has a surface area of 42.14 cm² $(6×2.65×2.65$, correct to 4 SF) and a volume of 18.61 cm³ $(2.65×2.65×2.65$, correct to 4 SF).

Prism (volumes only)

A prism is a solid shape with a uniform cross-sectional area (same shape all the way through).
   Volume of a prism=cross-sectional area×width

1 Triangular prism—see Fig. 3.12.

Volume of triangular prism = $\frac{1}{2} \times$ base length × height × width of prism

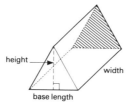

Fig. 3.12 *Triangular prism; cross section shaded*

2 Irregular prism—see Fig. 3.13.

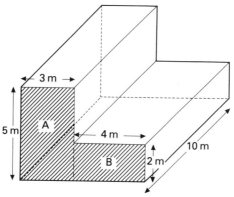

Fig. 3.13 *Irregular prism; cross section shaded*

★ Divide up the cross-section and find the individual areas.
★ Sum the individual areas, e.g. A+B.
★ Volume of prism = area of cross-section × width

Example:
Area of rectangle A = 5 m × 3 m = 15 m^2

37

Area of rectangle B = 4 m × 2 m = 8 m^2
Total area of cross-section = 23 m^2 (15 + 8)
Volume of prism = 23 m^2 × 10 m = 230 m^3

Cylinder (circular prism)

See Fig. 3.14.

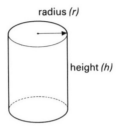

radius (r)

height (h)

Fig. 3.14 *Cylinder*

1 Surface area = area of cylinder base and top + curved area
$$= 2\pi r^2 + 2\pi rh$$
$$= 2\pi r(r + h)$$
2 Volume = area of base (cross-section) × height
$$= \pi r^2 h$$

Example: A cylinder of radius 8 cm and height 20 cm has a surface area of 1408 cm^2 (2 × 3.142 × 8 × 28, correct to 4 SF) and a volume of 4022 cm^3 (3.142 × 8 × 8 × 20, correct to 4 SF).

Pyramid (square-based)

See Fig. 3.15.
1 Surface area = area of base + 4 × area of a triangular face
$$= (\text{base length})^2 + 4 \times \tfrac{1}{2} \times \text{base length} \times \text{slant height}$$
$$= a^2 + 2al$$
$$= a(a + 2l)$$
2 Volume = $\tfrac{1}{3}$ × base area × vertical height
$$= \tfrac{1}{3}a^2 h$$

38

Example: A square-based pyramid has a base length of 12 cm and a vertical height of 8 cm.

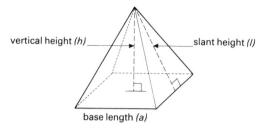

Fig. 3.15 *Pyramid*

1 It follows that the slant height is 10 cm (see theorem of Pythagoras, page 119).
2 Surface area of the pyramid is 384 cm² (12×(12+2×10)) and the volume is 384 cm³ ($\frac{1}{3}$×12×12×8).
3 It is just a coincidence that the surface area and volume have the same numerical result.

Cone (circular-based pyramid)
See Fig. 3.16.

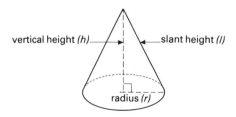

Fig. 3.16 *Cone*

1 Surface area = area of base circle + curved area

$$=\pi r^2 + \pi rl$$
$$=\pi r(r+l)$$

2 Volume = $\frac{1}{3} \times$ base area $\times$ vertical height
$$=\frac{1}{3}\pi r^2 h$$

Example: A cone with base radius of 5 cm and slant height of 13 cm has a total surface area of 282.8 cm² (3.142×5×(5+13), correct to 4 SF), and a volume of 314.2 cm³ ($\frac{1}{3}$×3.142×5×5×12, where the vertical height of 12 cm is calculated by the use of the theorem of Pythagoras).

Note: an open cone is a cone which has no base circle.

Sphere
See Fig. 3.17.

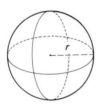

Fig. 3.17 *Sphere*

1 Surface area = $4 \times \pi \times$ (radius)²
$$=4\pi r^2$$

2 Volume = $\frac{4}{3} \times \pi \times$ (radius)³
$$=\frac{4\pi r^3}{3}$$

Example: A sphere with radius 15 cm has a surface area of 2828 cm² (4×3.142×15×15, correct to 4SF) and a volume of 14140 cm³ (4×3.142×15×15×15÷3, correct to 4 SF).

Note: half of a sphere, known as a hemisphere, has a surface area of $3\pi r^2$, and a volume of $\frac{2}{3}\pi r^3$.

Tessellations

1   A plane figure is said to **tessellate** if it will fill the entire plane, without leaving any gaps between the shape and using only the shape of the plane figure.

2   Any **triangle** or **quadrilateral** will tessellate. There are often various tessellation patterns which a particular figure may make (see Fig. 3.18).

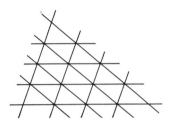

Fig. 3.18 *Tessellation of triangles*

3   Of the regular polygons, only the **equilateral triangle**, **square** and **hexagon** will tessellate (see Fig. 3.19).

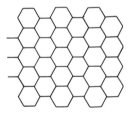

Fig. 3.19 *Tessellation of regular hexagons*

4 RATIO, SCALE AND VARIATION

Ratio

1 A **ratio** gives a comparison between quantities and helps to decide the proportional size of each.
2 The ratio 2:3 (two to three) means that a quantity is divided into five $(2+3)$ equal sections and reassembled into two parts, one containing 2 sections, the other containing 3 sections.

Example: If £50 is divided in the ratio 2:3 this will produce £20 and £30 since each section is worth £10 $(£50 \div 5)$.

Example: If 240 g is divided in the ratio 3:4:5 this will produce 60 g, 80 g and 100 g. Each section is a twelfth of 240 g $(3+4+5=12)$, giving:
$$\tfrac{3}{12} \times 240\,\text{g} = 60\,\text{g}; \quad \tfrac{4}{12} \times 240\,\text{g} = 80\,\text{g}; \quad \tfrac{5}{12} \times 240\,\text{g} = 100\,\text{g}$$

3 Ratio expressions may be **simplified** in much the same way as fractions can be cancelled.
   ★ 16:24 is identical to 8:12 which is identical to 4:6 and 2:3
   ★ 2:3 is the simplest form of the ratio 16:24
4 It is necessary to work in identical units of measurement to find the ratio of two quantities. The ratio of 25p to £3 is 25:300, which is 1:12 in its simplest form.

Scale

Map scales
1 A map scale of 1:50 000 means that a length measured on the map is 50 000 times smaller than the corresponding distance measured on the ground.

   1 cm on the map $\equiv$ 50 000 cm on the ground
   $\equiv$ 500 m on the ground
   $\equiv \tfrac{1}{2}$ km on the ground

2 Similarly, a distance measured on the ground is 50 000 times larger than a corresponding length measured on the map.

$$2\,\text{km on the ground} \equiv \frac{2}{50\,000}\,\text{km on the map}$$
$$\equiv \frac{2\,000}{50\,000}\,\text{m} = \frac{2}{50}\,\text{m on the map}$$

$$\equiv \frac{200}{50} \text{cm} = 4 \text{cm on the map}$$

Scale models

A scale model built to a scale of 1:10 means that all lengths on the real object are scaled down by a factor of 10 for the model.

Real object measurement	Scale model measurement
20 cm	2 cm
1 m (100 cm)	10 cm
3 cm	3 mm

Scale factors

If the lengths of a cuboid are doubled ($\times 2$), then the surface area becomes four times as large ($\times 4$), and the volume becomes eight times as large ($\times 8$) (see Fig. 4.1).

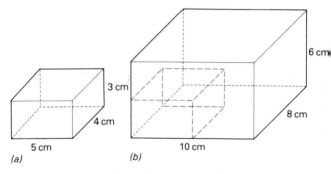

Fig. 4.1 (a) Surface area = $94 \, cm^2$; volume = $60 \, cm^3$. (b) Lengths doubled; surface area = $376 \, cm^2$; volume = $480 \, cm^3$

This chart shows the comparison between length, area and volume scale factors:

Length scale factor	Area scale factor	Volume scale factor
$\times 2$	$\times 4\ (2^2)$	$\times 8\ (2^3)$
$\times 3$	$\times 9\ (3^2)$	$\times 27\ (3^3)$
$\times 10$	$\times 100\ (10^2)$	$\times 1000\ (10^3)$
$\times\frac{1}{2}$	$\times\frac{1}{4}\ (\frac{1}{2}^2)$	$\times\frac{1}{8}\ (\frac{1}{2}^3)$
$\times n$	$\times n^2$	$\times n^3$

Variation

Direct proportion
Two quantities are in direct proportion to each other if an
increase in one results in the same proportional increase in the
other. Likewise for decreases. For example, if one quantity
doubles in size, then the other quantity also doubles in size if the
quantities are in direct proportion to each other.

Example: The cost of 2 m of cloth is £5. Therefore the cost of 4 m
of similar cloth is £10, i.e. the cost of the cloth is directly
proportional to its length.

In general terms, we write:

cost $\propto$ length   or   cost = constant number × length

$c \propto l$ $c = kl$

Inverse proportion
Two quantities are inversely proportional to each other if an
increase in one results in a decrease (by the same factor) in the
other, e.g. if one quantity trebles in size, then the other quantity
is decreased by one-third of its size if the two quantities are
inversely proportional to each other.

Example: If p is inversely proportional to q, and p is 5 when q is
12, find q when p is 15.

$p = 5$ $q = 12$
$p = 15$ $\therefore q = 4$
$(\times 3)$ $(\div 3)$

In general terms, we write:

$$p \propto \frac{1}{q} \text{ or } p = \frac{k}{q}$$

where k is a constant number.

Example: If y varies inversely to the square of x, and $y=9$ when $x=2$, find y when $x=1\frac{1}{2}$.

Firstly we are given that $y \propto \frac{1}{x^2}$ which means that $y = \frac{k}{x^2}$, where k is a constant. Using the fact that $y=9$ when $x=2$ gives:

$$9 = \frac{k}{4} \quad \therefore k = 36$$

Therefore the relationship between y and x can be expressed as:

$$y = \frac{36}{x^2}$$

When $x = 1\frac{1}{2}$, $y = \frac{36}{2\frac{1}{4}} = 16$.

5 PERCENTAGE

Fractional meaning

1 **Percentage** means 'out of one hundred', so it is possible to write a percentage as a fraction: 15 per cent (written as 15%) means 15 out of a hundred, or $\frac{15}{100}$.

2 For any fraction:
   fraction $\times 100 =$ percentage

3 For any percentage:
   percentage $\div 100 =$ fraction

4 The following results are worth remembering:

   ★ $10\% = \frac{10}{100} = \frac{1}{10}$

   ★ $25\% = \frac{25}{100} = \frac{1}{4}$

   ★ $33\frac{1}{3}\% = \frac{33\frac{1}{3}}{100} = \frac{1}{3}$

   ★ $50\% = \frac{50}{100} = \frac{1}{2}$

   ★ $66\frac{2}{3}\% = \frac{66\frac{2}{3}}{100} = \frac{2}{3}$

   ★ $75\% = \frac{75}{100} = \frac{3}{4}$

5 To find the percentage of a given quantity, the required percentage is converted to a fraction:

   ★ 15% of £200 is $\frac{15}{100} \times \frac{200}{1} = £30$

   ★ 37% of £100 is $\frac{37}{100} \times \frac{100}{1} = £37$

Decimal equivalent

Notation
The first two decimal places represent the hundredths in a

number, giving an alternative way of expressing a percentage:

$$0.37 = \frac{37}{100} = 37\%$$
$$0.895 = 89.5\%$$
$$0.7 = 70\%$$
$$0.07 = 7\%$$

It is convenient to use the decimal equivalent of a percentage when working with a calculator.

Decimal equivalent method of calculating percentages

To find the percentage of a given quantity, the required percentage is converted to a decimal number:

15% of £36 is $0.15 \times £36 = £5.40$

$37\frac{1}{2}\%$ of £4.96 is $0.375 \times £4.96 = £1.86$

Percentage calculations

Expressing a quantity as a percentage of another quantity

1   To express one quantity as a percentage of another quantity the two amounts are written as a fraction and then converted to a percentage.

Example: A quantity of 8 g expressed as a percentage of 25 g is calculated as follows:

$$\frac{8}{25} \times 100\% = 32\%$$

2   It is important that the two quantities are expressed in the same units of measurement.

Example: A time of 12 minutes expressed as a percentage of 1 hour is calculated as follows:

$$\frac{12}{60} \times 100\% = 20\%$$

Percentage change

1   To **increase** by a percentage, the original amount we start with is taken to be 100%.

Example: To increase £4 by 20% we know that the result will be

120% (100+20) of the original amount, so the calculation is:

$$\frac{120}{100}\times\pounds4=\pounds4.80 \text{ or } 1.20\times\pounds4=\pounds4.80$$

2 To **decrease** by a percentage, the original amount we start with is again taken to be 100%.

Example: To decrease 32 kg by 8% we know that the result will be 92% (100−8) of the original amount, so the calculation is:

$$\frac{92}{100}\times32\,kg=29.44\,kg \text{ or } 0.92\times32\,kg=29.44\,kg$$

Profit and loss
1 The difference between the cost price and the selling price of an item is called the **profit**.
2 If the selling price is less than the cost price, then this difference is called the **loss**.
3 Profit or loss is usually expressed as a percentage of the cost price.

Example: A merchant buys potatoes at £2.50 per sack, and sells them for £3.50 per sack. Find his profit as a percentage of the cost price.

Profit=£3.50−£2.50=£1.00

Percentage profit=$\frac{100}{250}\times100\%=40\%$ (working in pence)

Example: A car owner sells his car for £2000. It originally cost him £3600. Find his loss as a percentage of the cost price.

Loss=£3600−£2000=£1600

Percentage loss=$\frac{1600}{3600}\times100\%=44\frac{4}{9}\%$

Simple interest
1 When money is borrowed or invested the amount involved is called the **principal**.
2 The charge for borrowing, or the payment for investing, is called the **interest**.
3 The total amount of interest, I, on a principal, P, for a period of T years at a rate of interest $R\%$ per year is given by:

$$I=\frac{PRT}{100}$$

4 This formula may be rearranged to make any one of the four variables the subject, as follows:

$$P = \frac{100I}{RT} \qquad R = \frac{100I}{PT} \qquad T = \frac{100I}{PR}$$

5 The value of an investment at simple interest at the end of any year is given by Amount = Principal + Interest.

Example: Find the value of an investment of £1500 at a simple interest rate at $7\frac{1}{2}\%$ per year for 5 years.

The interest gained is:

$$\frac{1500 \times 7\frac{1}{2} \times 5}{100} = £562.50.$$

The value of the investment at the end of 5 years is:

£1500 + £562.50 = £2062.50

6 ALGEBRA

Use of letters

Unknown numbers

1 If the numbers in a relationship are unknown, then letters are often used to represent them.

2 The result of an unknown number being doubled may be expressed as $2n$, where n is the unknown number.

3 The result of two unknown numbers being subtracted may be expressed as $n-t$, where n and t are letters representing the unknown numbers.

4 It follows that, by a process of **simplification**:
   * $n+n=2n$
   * $n+n+n=3n$
   * $2n+3n=5n$
   * $5n-3n=2n$

5 Note that $n+t$ cannot be simplified algebraically.

Formula construction

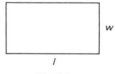

Fig. 6.1

The area of a rectangle with unknown dimensions may be expressed by the **formula**:

Area $=l\times w$

where l and w are letters representing the unknown numbers of length-units and width-units of the rectangle (see Fig. 6.1). This is usually written without the multiplication sign:

$A=lw$

where A is a letter representing the number of square units of the rectangle's area. The area of a square would be $l\times l$ or l^2, where l

is the length of one of the sides of the square.

It follows that, by a further process of **simplification**:

1 $n \times n = n^2$

2 $n \times n \times n = n^3$

3 $n^2 \times n^3 = n \times n \times n \times n \times n = n^5$

4 $n^5 \div n^3 = \dfrac{\not{n} \times \not{n} \times \not{n} \times n \times n}{\not{n} \times \not{n} \times \not{n}} = n^2$

5 Note that nt cannot be simplified algebraically.

Sequences and function rules

Matchsticks can be arranged to make a number of triangles in a row (see Fig. 6.2).

Fig. 6.2

Number of triangles, t	1	2	3	t	$\frac{1}{2}(m-1)$
Number of matches, m	3	5	7	$2t+1$	m

From the chart it will be seen that 3 triangles require 7 matches.

1 We can work out the required number of matches required for any number of triangles:

t triangles require $2t+1$ matches

$2t+1=m$ is called the **function rule**.

2 We can work out the number of triangles which can be made from any number of matches:

m matches will make $\frac{1}{2}(m-1)$ triangles

$\frac{1}{2}(m-1)=t$ is called the **inverse function rule**.

3 To produce the inverse function rule, the function rule is **rearranged**.

 ★ The method is to find the inverse operations and combine these in reverse order, as follows:

51

$2t+1=m$

* Last operation $+1$ which has an inverse operation of -1:
  $2t=m-1$
* First operation $\times 2$ which has an inverse operation of $\times\frac{1}{2}$:
  $t=\frac{1}{2}(m-1)$

Example: Make r the subject of $C=2\pi r$.
$2\pi r=C$

The operation is $\times 2\pi$ which has an inverse operation of $\times\frac{1}{2\pi}$:

$$r=C\times\frac{1}{2\pi}=\frac{C}{2\pi}$$

Example: Make m the subject of $y=mx+c$.
$mx+c=y$

Last operation $+c$ which has an inverse operation of $-c$:
$mx=y-c$
First operation $\times x$ which has an inverse operation of $\times\frac{1}{x}$:

$$m=(y-c)\times\frac{1}{x}=\frac{y-c}{x}$$

Example: Make n the subject of $t=\frac{a(n+3)}{2}$

$$\frac{a(n+3)}{2}=t$$

Last operation $\times\frac{1}{2}$ which has an inverse operation of $\times 2$:
$a(n+3)=2t$

Next operation $\times a$ which has an inverse operation of $\times\frac{1}{a}$:

$$n+3=\frac{2t}{a}$$

First operation $+3$ which has an inverse operation of -3:
$$n=\frac{2t}{a}-3$$

Substitution

If the function rule is $m=2t+1$, we can find m by substituting a number for the letter t, e.g. if $t=30$ then $m=2\times30+1=61$. When a formula contains many letters, more than one substitution will be necessary.

Example: Find the value of p if $p=ab^2+c$ and $a=4$, $b=-3$ and $c=-7$.

$$p=ab^2+c=4\times(-3)^2+(-7)=4\times9-7=36-7=29$$

Relations and functions

Relations

1 A **relation** such as 'is larger than' may be illustrated by a mapping diagram for a particular set of numbers.
2 The set to be considered is called the **domain set**, which might be a particular set of numbers such as $\{1, 2, 3, 4\}$.
3 The relation connects the members of the domain set to the members of a **co-domain set**, such as $\{1, 2, 3, 4\}$ (see Fig. 6.3).

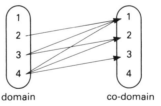

Fig. 6.3 *The relation 'is larger than'*

4 The **range** of the relation is a subset of the co-domain which has elements with mapping arrows pointing towards them, such as $\{1, 2, 3\}$ in this case.

Functions

A **function** is a **one-to-one** or a **many-to-one** relation which relates every member of the domain set to the co-domain set.

1 One-to-one, e.g. the doubling function $f(x) \rightarrow 2x$ (see Fig. 6.4).

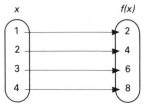

Fig. 6.4 *Doubling function*

2 Many-to-one, e.g. the squaring function $f(x) \rightarrow x^2$ (see Fig. 6.5).

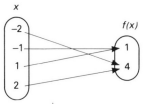

Fig. 6.5 *Squaring function*

Inverse functions

An **inverse function** is a function which relates every member of the range to one and only one member of the domain set. Note that only one-to-one mappings have an inverse function.

Example: The arrow diagram in Fig. 6.6 shows the function $f(x) \rightarrow 2x+1$ and the inverse function.

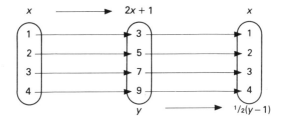

$f(y) \mapsto \frac{1}{2}(y-1)$ is the inverse function of $f(x)$. The inverse function $f(y)$ is usually written as $f^{-1}(x)$.

Hint: to calculate an inverse function for $f(x)$, let $y = f(x)$ and rearrange the formula to make x the subject. This gives the inverse function:

1   $y = 2x + 1$ Function
2   $x = \frac{1}{2}(y-1)$ Inverse function

Composite functions

1   The function $f(x) \mapsto 4x - 3$ is made up from the two simple functions:

     $g(x) \mapsto 4x$ and $h(x) \mapsto x - 3$

     i.e. the **multiply by four** function and the **subtract three** function.

2   The **composite function** $f(x)$ is $h(g(x))$ or $hg(x)$.
3   Note the order:

     ★   function g applied first;
     ★   followed by h.

4   The opposite order would produce $gh(x)$ which is

     $4(x-3) = 4x - 12$

Example: If $f(x) \mapsto x - 5$ and $g(x) \mapsto 3x$, then $fg(x) \mapsto 3x - 5$ and $gf(x) \mapsto 3(x-5) = 3x - 15$.

5   In general $fg(x) \neq gf(x)$.

Algebraic expressions

Linear expressions
1 $2n+3$ is a **linear expression** in n.
2 The letter n is an unknown number, or it may represent a variety of numbers, in which case it is called a **variable**.
3 There are no terms in n^2 or higher powers in a linear expression.

Factorization of linear expressions
1 $2n+4=2(n+2)$ for all values of n.
2 In this case, 2 is said to be a **common factor**.
3 The act of forming a bracket with the common factor so that the linear expression is the product of the bracket and the common factor is called **factorization**.

It follows that:

General case	Particular case
$an+a=a(n+1)$	$3n+3=3(n+1)$
$an+bn=n(a+b)$	$3n+4n=n(3+4)=7n$

where a, b and n are real numbers.

Quadratic expressions
1 $3n^2+4n-7$ is a **quadratic expression** in n.
2 The letter n is a variable number.
3 In this case 3 is the coefficient of n^2, 4 is the coefficient of n and -7 is the constant.
4 A quadratic expression always has a non-zero coefficient of n^2.
5 There are no terms in n^3 or higher powers in a quadratic expression.

Factorization of quadratic expressions
To factorize a quadratic the expression needs to be written as the product of two linear expressions in the variable letter, in this case:
$$3n^2+4n-7=(3n+7)(n-1)$$

Example: See Fig. 6.7.

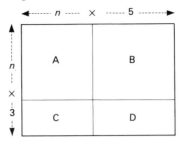

Fig. 6.7

1 The length of the rectangle is $n+5$.
2 The width of the rectangle is $n+3$.
3 Area of region A is $n\times n=n^2$.
4 Area of region B is $5\times n=5n$.
5 Area of region C is $3\times n=3n$.
6 Area of region D is $5\times 3=15$.
7 Total area of the rectangle $=n^2+5n+3n+15$
$$=n^2+8n+15$$
$$=(n+5)(n+3)$$
8 The factorized form of the quadratic $n^2+8n+15$ is $(n+5)(n+3)$.
9 Note that the sum of 5 and 3 is 8 (coefficient of n) and the product of 5 and 3 is 15 (constant term).
10 This is true for quadratics which have 1 as the coefficient of n^2, and this method is used as a technique for factorizing a quadratic expression.

Example: Factorize $x^2+3x-10$.

Two numbers which add to make $+3$ and multiply together to make -10 are $+5$ and -2, so it follows that:
$$x^2+3x-10=(x+5)(x-2)$$

Example: Factorize $3n^2+2n-8$.

1 One method is to multiply the coefficient of n^2 by the constant and then find the factors of this result which add to make the coefficient of n.
  ★ In this case $3 \times -8 = -24$ and $+6 + -4 = +2$.
  ★ Hence $3n^2+2n-8 = 3n^2+6n-4n-8$.
2 Then factorize in pairs, being careful with negative factors, to give:
$$3n^2+6n-4n-8 = 3n(n+2)-4(n+2)$$
$$= (n+2)(3n-4)$$
from the distributive law (see page 18).

The difference of two squares
1 If the product $(a+b)(a-b)$ is distributed, the following useful result is found:
$$(a+b)(a-b) = a(a-b)+b(a-b)$$
$$= a^2-ab+ab-b^2$$
$$= a^2-b^2$$
2 It follows that:
$$23 \times 17 = (20+3)(20-3)$$
$$= 20^2-3^2$$
$$= 400-9$$
$$= 391$$
3 The following illustrate the procedure for **factorizing the difference of two squares:**
  ★ $a^2-b^2 = (a+b)(a-b)$
  ★ $4-n^2 = (2+n)(2-n)$
  ★ $9t^2-1 = (3t+1)(3t-1)$
  ★ $p^4-16 = (p^2+4)(p^2-4)$

Algebraic fractions
1 Combining and simplifying algebraic fractions follows the procedures for combining and simplifying numerical fractions.
2 To add or subtract, a common denominator is required:
$$\frac{a}{b} + \frac{c}{d} = \frac{ad}{bd} + \frac{bc}{bd} = \frac{ad+bc}{bd}$$

58

$$\frac{3}{p} - \frac{1}{2p} = \frac{6}{2p} - \frac{1}{2p} = \frac{5}{2p}$$

3 Common factors in the numerator and denominator may be cancelled:

$$\frac{rs}{st} = \frac{r}{t} \quad \text{and} \quad \frac{ab+ac}{bx+cx} = \frac{a(b+c)}{x(b+c)} = \frac{a}{x}$$

4 Multiplication and division:

$$\frac{a}{b} \times \frac{a}{c} = \frac{a^2}{bc} \quad \text{and} \quad \frac{a}{b} \div \frac{a}{c} = \frac{a}{b} \times \frac{c}{a} = \frac{c}{b}$$

5 Writing an algebraic expression as a single fraction in its simplest form may require a combination of algebraic techniques.

★ $\dfrac{a}{a-t} - \dfrac{t}{a+t}$ has a common denominator of $(a-t)(a+t)$.

★ This gives:

$$\frac{a(a+t)}{(a-t)(a+t)} - \frac{t(a-t)}{(a+t)(a-t)}$$

★ which reduces to:

$$\frac{a^2+at-at+t^2}{(a-t)(a+t)} = \frac{a^2+t^2}{a^2-t^2}$$

7 EQUATIONS AND INEQUATIONS

Methods of solution

Both algebraic methods and graphical methods may be used to solve equations. The algebraic methods follow in this chapter. Graphical methods will be found in the next chapter on coordinates.

Linear equations

A **linear equation** is a mathematical statement of equality with one unknown number expressed as a letter, such as n. No powers of the letter, such as n^2, n^3, etc., are used in a linear equation. In solving the equation, operations performed on one side of the equation, on the right or left of the equals sign, are balanced by the same operation performed on the other side of the equation.

1 $3p-4=8$ is a linear equation in p.
  * It follows that $3p=12$ when 4 is added to both sides of the equation.
  * This leads to $p=4$ when both sides of the equation are divided by 3, thus giving the solution of the equation.

2 $4s+5=7s-1$ is a linear equation in s.
  * $5=3s-1$ subtracting $4s$ from both sides.
  * $6=3s$ adding 1 to both sides.
  * $2=s$ or $s=2$ dividing both sides by 3.

Linear inequations

A **linear inequation** is a mathematical statement of inequality with one unknown number expressed as a letter. These inequality signs are used:

1 $<$ less than
2 $\leq$ less than or equal to
3 $>$ greater than
4 $\geq$ greater than or equal to

In solving the inequality, operations performed on one side of the inequality sign must be balanced by the same numerical operation being performed on the other side. It is important that care is taken with multiplication and division operations since these may change the direction of the inequality sign.

Example: What is the solution to the inequality $8q + 3 > 19$?

1 $8q > 16$ subtracting 3 from both sides of the inequality sign.
2 $q > 2$ dividing both sides by 8.

Example: Find all the positive non-zero integral solutions which satisfy the inequality $15 - t \leqslant 21 - 3t$.

1 Add $3t$ to both sides $\qquad$ $15 + 2t \leqslant 21$
2 Subtract 15 from both sides $\qquad$ $2t \leqslant 6$
3 Divide both sides by 2 $\qquad$ $t \leqslant 3$
4 The set of positive non-zero integral solutions is $\{1, 2, 3\}$.

Simultaneous equations (two unknowns)

Elimination procedure
This pair of equations has two unknown numbers represented by the letters x and y. The values of these unknown numbers in the first equation are identical to the values in the second equation, which is why they are called **simultaneous equations**.

$$2x + 3y = 24$$
$$x - 4y = 1$$

In the elimination procedure the coefficients of one of the unknowns are equated and eliminated by either adding or subtracting the two equations:

$$2x + 3y = 24$$
$$2x - 8y = 2$$

The second equation has been multiplied by 2 to make the coefficients of x in both equations identical. The unknown, x, is eliminated by subtraction:

$$11y = 22$$

Dividing both sides by 11 gives:

$$y = 2$$

Substitute $y = 2$ in the first (or second) equation:

$$2x + 6 = 24$$
$$2x = 18 \qquad \text{subtracting 6 from both sides}$$
$$x = 9 \qquad \text{dividing both sides by 2}$$

Hence the solution to the pair of simultaneous equations is:

$x=9$ and $y=2$

Note: sometimes both equations need to be multiplied by different numbers to equate the coefficients of one of the unknowns.

Substitution procedure

In the substitution procedure one of the equations is rearranged to make one of the unknowns the subject. This is then substituted in the remaining equation. Using the previous example, the second equation may be rearranged to make x the subject:

$x-4y=1$ becomes $x=4y+1$

Substituting $4y+1$ for x in the first equation gives:

$2(4y+1)+3y=24$

$\qquad 8y+2+3y=24 \qquad$ expanding the bracket

$\qquad 11y+2=24$

$\qquad 11y=22 \qquad$ subtracting 2 from both sides

$\qquad y=2 \qquad$ dividing both sides by 11

Substitute $y=2$ in the first equation:

$\qquad 2x+6=24$

$\qquad 2x=18$

$\qquad x=9$

The solution is:

$\qquad x=9$ and $y=2$

For a **matrix method** of solving simultaneous equations see Chapter 9.

Quadratic equations

A **quadratic equation** is a mathematical statement of equality with one unknown expressed as a letter in the form of a quadratic expression, e.g. $d^2-2d-15=0$ is a quadratic equation in d. The factorization procedure (see Chapter 6) is used to solve many quadratic equations.

1 It will be understood that if $ab=0$ then either a or b must be zero.

2 Similarly, if $(c-3)(c-4)=0$ then either $c-3$ or $c-4$ must be zero.

3 In this case it follows that $c-3=0$ gives $c=3$ and $c-4=0$ gives $c=4$.

Example: Solve the quadratic equation $d^2 - 2d - 15 = 0$.

This quadratic equation in d may be factorized into:
   $(d-5)(d+3) = 0$
Hence:
   $d-5=0 \quad d=5$
   $d+3=0 \quad d=-3$
The solution is:
   $d=5$ or $d=-3$

Example: Solve the quadratic equation $3e^2 + 2 = 7e$.

This quadratic equation in e may be rearranged into $3e^2 - 7e + 2 = 0$ and then factorized into:
   $(3e-1)(e-2) = 0$
Hence:
   $3e-1=0 \quad 3e=1 \quad e=\tfrac{1}{3}$
or:
   $e-2=0 \quad e=2$
The solution is:
   $e=\tfrac{1}{3}$ or $e=2$

The **general equation of a quadratic** is $ax^2 + bx + c = 0$ where x is the unknown and a, b and c are real numbers. The solution to this quadratic equation is given by the formula:

$$x = \frac{-b \pm \sqrt{b^2 - 4ac}}{2a}$$

It is convenient to use this formula if the quadratic expression does not factorize.

Example: Solve the quadratic equation $3x^2 - 2x - 4 = 0$ giving the answers correct to two decimal places.

It will be seen that $a=3$, $b=-2$ and $c=-4$

$$x = \frac{-(-2) \pm \sqrt{(-2)^2 - 4(3)(-4)}}{2 \times 3}$$

$$= \frac{2 \pm \sqrt{52}}{6} = \frac{2 + 7.211}{6} \text{ or } \frac{2 - 7.211}{6}$$

$x = 1.54$ or $x = -0.87$

8 COORDINATES

Cartesian coordinates

1 The **horizontal axis** is called the **x axis** and has the equation $y=0$.
2 The **vertical axis** is called the **y axis** and has the equation $x=0$.
3 The axes divide the plane into four quarters, called **quadrants**.
4 The axes cross at the **origin**.
5 The axes are divided up into equal sections and are numbered as shown in Fig. 8.1.

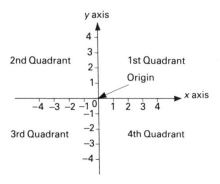

Fig. 8.1 *The axes of Cartesian coordinates*

6 The **coordinates of a point** give the horizontal distance from the origin followed by the vertical distance from the origin.
  ★ The coordinates of the origin are $(0,0)$.
  ★ The coordinates of a point in the 1st quadrant have the form (x,y).
  ★ The coordinates of a point in the 2nd quadrant have the form $(-x,y)$.

- ★ The coordinates of a point in the 3rd quadrant have the form $(-x, -y)$.
- ★ The coordinates of a point in the 4th quadrant have the form $(x, -y)$.

In each case x and y are positive real numbers.

7 The **midpoint** between two points with coordinates (a,b) and (c,d) is:
$$\left(\frac{a+c}{2}, \frac{b+d}{2} \right)$$

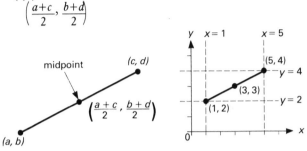

Straight lines

1 **Horizontal lines**, parallel to the x axis, have equations of the form $y=k$, where k is a real number.

2 **Vertical lines**, parallel to the y axis, have equations of the form $x=k$, where k is a real number.

3 The **equation of a straight line** gives the relation between the x values and the y values of the coordinate pairs which form all the points on the line.

4 The **general equation of a straight line** is $y=mx+c$, where m is a number representing the gradient or steepness of the line and c is a number which indicates the y axis point of intersection $(0,c)$.

5 The **gradient** of a straight line is constant and is measured as:
$$m = \frac{\text{Vertical displacement}}{\text{Horizontal displacement}}$$

6 Positive and negative gradients are illustrated in Fig. 8.3.

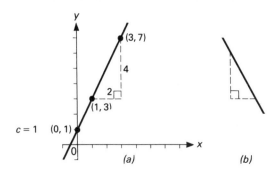

Fig. 8.3 (a) Positive gradient: m=$\frac{4}{2}$=2; the equation of this line is

y=2x+1. (b) Negative gradient

7 The straight line with equation $y=4x-3$ has a gradient of 4
   and a y axis intersection point of $(0,-3)$.

8 The **gradient** of a straight line going through the two points
   (a,b) and (c,d) is:

   $$\frac{\text{Vertical displacement (increase in } y)}{\text{Horizontal displacement (increase in } x)} = \frac{d-b}{c-a}$$

Example: Find the gradient of the line joining $(2,1)$ and $(5,10)$.

Using the above formula:

$$m=\frac{10-1}{5-1}=\frac{9}{3}=3$$

The gradient of the line is 3 (or 3 in 1).

9 The **equation** of a straight line going through the two points
   (a,b) and (c,d) is:

   $$\frac{y-b}{d-b}=\frac{x-a}{c-a}$$

   or $y-b=m(x-a)$ where m is calculated as above.

66

Example: Find the equation of the line joining $(2,1)$ and $(5,10)$.

Using the above formula:
$$\frac{y-1}{10-1} = \frac{x-2}{5-2}$$
which gives $y-1=3(x-2)$ when multiplied through by 9. This may be rearranged into:
$$y=3x-5$$

10 The straight line with equation $x+y=7$ (which can be written as $y=-x+7$) has a negative gradient of -1, and passes through the points $(0,7)$ and $(7,0)$, as shown in Fig. 8.4.

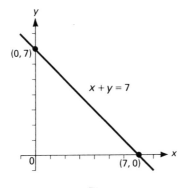

Fig. 8.4

11 Lines with a **negative gradient** slope from the top left to the bottom right. Lines with a **positive gradient** slope from the top right to the bottom left.

12 The **intersection point** of two straight lines provides an alternative method of solving a pair of simultaneous equations.

Example: Find the point of intersection of the lines with equations
$$y=3x-2$$

$$x+y=6$$

The first line has a gradient of 3 and goes through $(0,-2)$. The second line goes through $(6,0)$ and $(0,6)$. Each line is then plotted (see Fig. 8.5).

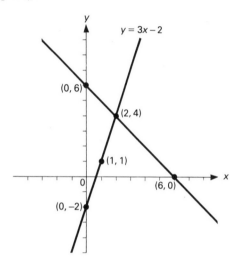

Fig. 8.5

The point of intersection is $(2,4)$, and this provides a solution to the simultaneous equations of $x=2$ and $y=4$.

13 The equation $2x+1=3x-2$ may be solved by finding the point of intersection of the two lines with equations:

$$y=2x+1$$
$$y=3x-2$$

Plotting the lines gives a point of intersection of $(3,7)$, and so the solution of the equation is $x=3$.

Coordinate areas

The **area** bounded between lines joining coordinate points may be calculated.

Example: Find the area of the triangle ABC (Fig. 8.6) with coordinates A (−3,4), B (5,1) and C (1,−2).

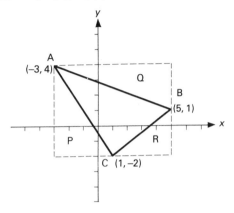

Fig. 8.6

1 If the triangle is enclosed in a rectangular box as shown, then the area of this box is 48 squares.
2 The areas of the surrounding right-angled triangles are calculated.
   ⋆ Area of triangle P is 12 squares.
   ⋆ Area of triangle Q is 12 squares.
   ⋆ Area of triangle R is 6 squares.
   The total area of triangles P, Q and R is 30 squares.
3 Therefore the area of triangle ABC is 48−30=18 squares.

The areas of other coordinate shapes and regions may be found by similar procedures.

Coordinate regions
Here the *unwanted* parts of a region are shaded out.
1   An inequality such as $-3<x\leq4$ may be used to describe a
    coordinate region.
2   The boundary lines of this region are $x=-3$ and $x=4$.
3   The line $x=-3$ is shown as a broken line since x is strictly
    greater than -3, and points on the line are not included as
    they do not satisfy the condition.
4   The line $x=4$ is shown as a continuous line since x is less than
    or equal to 4.
5   The infinite region is shown in Fig. 8.7

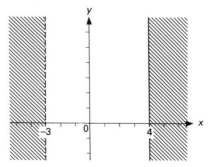

Fig. 8.7. *The infinite region*

Intersection of regions
1   These regions have a finite intersection:
    $$y\leq x, y\geq1, x+y\leq5$$
2   The boundary lines (all continuous) are:
    $$y=x, y=1, x+y=5$$
3   To check which side of the boundary line is to be shaded out,
    choose a point (x,y) on one side of the line and substitute the x
    and y values of the point in the inequality.
4   If the resulting statement is true shade the other side of the

boundary line, as the condition is satisfied. If the statement is false shade the same side of the boundary line as the chosen point, as the condition is not satisfied.

5 In this case consider the point $(1,2)$ marked in Fig. 8.8.
* For the region $y \leqslant x : 2 \leqslant 1$ is false, so shade this side.
* For the region $y \geqslant 1 : 2 \geqslant 1$ is true, so shade the other side.
* For the region $x+y \leqslant 5 : 1+2 \leqslant 5$ is true, so shade the other side of this boundary line.
* The finite region A represents the intersection of these three regions

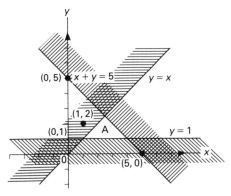

Fig. 8.8

Linear programming
Linear programming is a method of finding graphically a suitable solution set of values in an industrial or commercial problem involving restricting conditions (expressed as inequalities).

Example: A small factory makes two types of lamp-stand, the ordinary and the special. The ordinary lamp-stand requires 3 hours machine time and 1 hour in the finishing shop. The special version requires 2 hours machine time and 2 hours in the finishing shop. The profit on the ordinary lamp-stand is £5 and on the special lamp-stand £7. The factory machinery has a maximum capacity of 60 hours work a week. The craftsman in the finishing shop works for 40 hours a week. How many of each type of lamp-stand should the factory make each week to maximize profit, assuming demand exceeds supply.

1 Let the number of ordinary lamp-stands made each week be x and the number of special lamp-stands made each week be y.
2 The machine time for each ordinary lamp-stand is 3 hours; therefore the machine time for x ordinary lamp-stands is $3x$ hours.
3 The machine time for each special lamp-stand is 2 hours; therefore the machine time for y special lamp-stands is $2y$ hours.
4 The total amount of machine hours cannot exceed the maximum capacity of 60 hours a week. This leads to the first inequality:
   $3x+2y \leqslant 60$
5 The finishing shop time for each ordinary lamp-stand is 1 hour; therefore the finishing shop time for x ordinary lamp-stands is x hours.
6 The finishing shop time for each special lamp-stand is 2 hours; therefore the finishing shop time for y special lamp-stands is $2y$ hours.
7 The total amount of finishing shop time cannot exceed the maximum capacity of 40 hours a week. This leads to the second inequality:
   $x+2y \leqslant 40$
8 It is clear that x and y are not negative numbers, which gives two further inequalities:
   $x \geqslant 0$ and $y \geqslant 0$
9 The solution set is the intersection of these four regions:
   $3x+2y \leqslant 60, x+2y \leqslant 40, x \geqslant 0, y \geqslant 0$
10 The boundary lines (all continuous) are:
   $3x+2y=60, x+2y=40, x=0, y=0$
11 The line $3x+2y=60$ goes through the points $(0,30)$ and $(20,0)$.
12 The line $x+2y=40$ goes through the points $(0,20)$ and $(40,0)$.

13 The intersection of the regions is shown in Fig. 8.9.

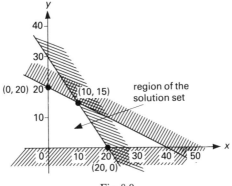

Fig. 8.9

14 We now find the profit equation.
  ★ The profit on each ordinary lamp-stand is £5.
  ★ The profit on x ordinary lamp-stands is £5x.
  ★ The profit on each special lamp-stand is £7.
  ★ The profit on y special lamp-stands is £7y.
  The total profit made each week will be £$(5x+7y)$.
15 The profit is maximized by making as many lamp-stands of
  the appropriate type as possible, but the solution point which
  is chosen must be within the solution set shown in Fig. 8.9.
16 We consider the extreme points of the solution set, which are
  (0,20), (10,15) and (20,0).

Point	Ordinary	Special	Profit	
(0,20)	0	20	£140	(5×0+7×20)
(10,15)	10	15	£155	(5×10+7×15)
(20,0)	20	0	£100	(5×20+7×0)

The maximum profit per week is £155 from the production of 10
ordinary and 15 special lamp-stands.

The parabola

1 The points which satisfy the relation $y = x^2$ trace out a curve called a **parabola** (see Fig. 8.10).

2 Some of the points on the parabola are given in this table:

x	−3	−2	−1	0	1	2	3
y	9	4	1	0	1	4	9

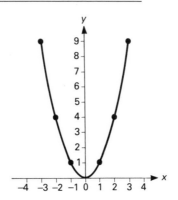

Fig. 8.10 *A parabola*

3 A quadratic relation such as $y = ax^2 + bx + c$, where a, b and c are real numbers, is the **equation of a parabola**.

4 A quadratic equation may be solved graphically by plotting the parabola and finding the points of intersection with the x axis.

Example: Solve the quadratic equation $x^2 - 2x - 3 = 0$.

The graphical method requires the plotting of the parabola $y = x^2 - 2x - 3$ (see Fig. 8.11). Some points are listed in this table:

x	−2	−1	0	1	2	3	4
y	5	0	−3	−4	−3	0	5

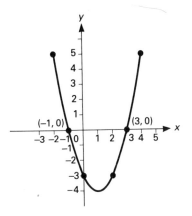

Fig. 8.11

When $x^2 - 2x - 3 = 0$, $y = 0$ (x axis). The intersection of the x axis with the parabola occurs at $(-1, 0)$ and $(3, 0)$. Hence, the solutions to the quadratic equation are $x = -1$ and $x = 3$.

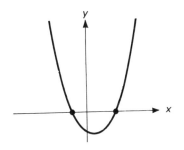

Fig. 8.12 *Parabola with two real roots*

5 A parabola of the form $y=ax^2+bx+c$ may not always have two real solutions (called roots).

⋆ If $b^2>4ac$ the quadratic has **two real roots** and the parabola cuts the x axis at two distinct points (see Fig. 8.12).

⋆ If $b^2=4ac$ the quadratic has **one** (repeated) **real root** and the parabola touches the x axis at one point (see Fig. 8.13).

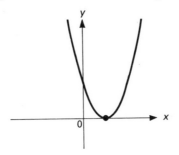

Fig. 8.13 *Parabola with one real root*

⋆ If $b^2<4ac$ the quadratic has **no real roots** and the parabola does not cut the x axis (see Fig. 8.14).

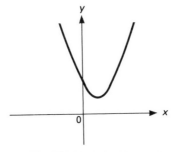

Fig. 8.14 *Parabola with no real roots*

6 The solution of **simultaneous equations** of the form $y=mx+k$ and $y=ax^2+bx+c$ may be found by plotting the straight line and the parabola represented by these equations on the same graph and finding the points of intersection. The points of intersection shown as (p,q) and (r,s) in Fig. 8.15 give the required simultaneous solutions.

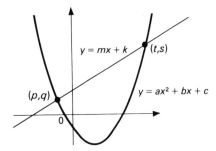

Fig. 8.15

9 MATRICES

Definitions

1 A **matrix** is an array of numbers.
2 A **row matrix** is a single row of numbers.
3 A **column matrix** is a single column of numbers.

Examples:

$$(3\ 4\ 2) \qquad \begin{pmatrix} 5 \\ 7 \end{pmatrix} \qquad \begin{pmatrix} 1 & 3 & 2 & 5 \\ 3 & -1 & 0 & 7 \\ 5 & -2 & -1 & 4 \end{pmatrix}$$

Row matrix   Column matrix 3×4 matrix

4 The **order of a matrix** is the number of rows in the matrix followed by the number of columns in the matrix. A 3×4 (three by four) matrix has three rows and four columns.
5 The numbers in a matrix are called its **elements**.
6 Two matrices are **identical** if the order of each matrix is the same and the corresponding elements are equal.
7 Two matrices are **conformable** if the number of columns in the first matrix is equal to the number of rows in the second matrix. A 3×4 matrix is conformable with a 4×2 matrix.

Addition of matrices
1 Only matrices of the same order may be added together.
2 For addition the corresponding elements in each matrix are added.
3 The answer matrix has the same order as the matrices which have been added.

Example:
$$\begin{pmatrix} 3 & 4 & 1 \\ 2 & 5 & 6 \end{pmatrix} + \begin{pmatrix} 1 & 2 & 7 \\ 0 & 4 & 1 \end{pmatrix} = \begin{pmatrix} 4 & 6 & 8 \\ 2 & 9 & 7 \end{pmatrix}$$
Matrix order: 2×3 2×3 2×3

Subtraction of matrices
1 Only matrices of the same order may be subtracted.
2 For subtraction the corresponding elements in each matrix are subtracted.

3 The answer matrix has the same order as the matrices which have been subtracted.

Example:
$$\begin{pmatrix} 4 & 0 \\ 3 & -2 \end{pmatrix} - \begin{pmatrix} 1 & 5 \\ 2 & -3 \end{pmatrix} = \begin{pmatrix} 3 & -5 \\ -3 & 1 \end{pmatrix}$$
Matrix order: 2×2 2×2 2×2

Multiplication

Multiplication of a matrix by a scalar
1 A **scalar** is a single number, integral or fractional.
2 Each element in a matrix is multiplied by the scalar.
3 The order of the matrix is not affected.

Example:
$$3 \begin{pmatrix} 1 & 0 \\ 2 & -1 \\ 3 & -2 \end{pmatrix} = \begin{pmatrix} 3 & 0 \\ 6 & -3 \\ 9 & -6 \end{pmatrix}$$

Multiplication of a row matrix by a column matrix
The number of elements in the row matrix must be the same as the number of elements in the column matrix. A number in turn in the row matrix is multiplied by a number in turn in the column matrix, and these products are summed to give a single numerical answer.

Example: A secretary posts 3 first-class letters, 10 second-class letters and 2 letters to Europe. This may be expressed as a row matrix:
$(3 \ 10 \ 2)$
The cost of these letters, in the respective order, is 17p, 13p and 22p. This may be expressed as a column matrix:
$$\begin{pmatrix} 17 \\ 13 \\ 22 \end{pmatrix}$$
The product of these conformable matrices is as follows:
$$(3 \ 10 \ 2) \begin{pmatrix} 17 \\ 13 \\ 22 \end{pmatrix} = 3 \times 17 + 10 \times 13 + 2 \times 22 = 225$$
Matrix order: 1×3 3×1 1×1

The result, which is a single number representing the total cost of postage, is £2.25.

Multiplication of matrices

1. Matrices have to be conformable for the operation of multiplication.
2. Each element of each row in the first matrix is multiplied by each element of each corresponding column in the second matrix.
3. Two conformable matrices of order $a \times b$ and $b \times c$ have a matrix product which is of order $a \times c$.

Example:

$$\begin{pmatrix} 1 & 2 & 3 \\ 3 & 4 & 1 \end{pmatrix} \begin{pmatrix} 5 \\ 0 \\ 2 \end{pmatrix} = \begin{pmatrix} 1 \times 5 + 2 \times 0 + 3 \times 2 \\ 3 \times 5 + 4 \times 0 + 1 \times 2 \end{pmatrix} = \begin{pmatrix} 11 \\ 17 \end{pmatrix}$$

Matrix order: 2×3 3×1 2×1

2×2 matrices

1. The **null**, or **zero**, matrix is $\begin{pmatrix} 0 & 0 \\ 0 & 0 \end{pmatrix}$. It is often represented by **O**. It acts as an additive identity:

$$\begin{pmatrix} 3 & 4 \\ 6 & 2 \end{pmatrix} + \begin{pmatrix} 0 & 0 \\ 0 & 0 \end{pmatrix} = \begin{pmatrix} 3 & 4 \\ 6 & 2 \end{pmatrix}$$

2. The **identity**, or **unit**, matrix is $\begin{pmatrix} 1 & 0 \\ 0 & 1 \end{pmatrix}$. It is often represented by **I**. It acts as a multiplicative identity:

$$\begin{pmatrix} 3 & 4 \\ 6 & 2 \end{pmatrix} \begin{pmatrix} 1 & 0 \\ 0 & 1 \end{pmatrix} = \begin{pmatrix} 3 & 4 \\ 6 & 2 \end{pmatrix}$$

3. For a matrix $\mathbf{A} = \begin{pmatrix} a & b \\ c & d \end{pmatrix}$, the value $ad - bc$ is called the **determinant** of matrix **A**. It is often represented by $\triangle$.

4. The **inverse** of matrix $\mathbf{A} = \begin{pmatrix} a & b \\ c & d \end{pmatrix}$ is this matrix of rearranged elements multiplied by the reciprocal of its determinant:

$$\frac{1}{\triangle} \begin{pmatrix} d & -b \\ -c & a \end{pmatrix}$$

It is symbolized by $\mathbf{A}^{-1}$.

Note: $\mathbf{A} \times \mathbf{A}^{-1} = \mathbf{I}$, i.e. the product of a matrix with its inverse (if it exists) is the identity matrix.

Example:

$$\frac{1}{\overline{1}}\begin{pmatrix}5 & 7\\2 & 3\end{pmatrix}\begin{pmatrix}3 & -7\\-2 & 5\end{pmatrix}=\begin{pmatrix}1 & 0\\0 & 1\end{pmatrix}$$

In this case $\triangle=1$

5 Matrix multiplication is used to find the **powers of matrices**:
$$\mathbf{A}\times\mathbf{A}=\mathbf{A}^2 \quad \mathbf{A}\times\mathbf{A}^2=\mathbf{A}^3 \quad \mathbf{A}^2\times\mathbf{A}^2=\mathbf{A}^4 \quad \mathbf{A}^2\times\mathbf{A}^3=\mathbf{A}^5 \text{ etc.}$$

6 In general, matrix multiplication is **not commutative**:
$$\mathbf{AB}\neq\mathbf{BA}$$

Example:

$$\mathbf{AB}=\begin{pmatrix}1 & 2\\3 & 4\end{pmatrix}\begin{pmatrix}5 & 1\\2 & 3\end{pmatrix}=\begin{pmatrix}9 & 7\\23 & 15\end{pmatrix}$$

$$\mathbf{BA}=\begin{pmatrix}5 & 1\\2 & 3\end{pmatrix}\begin{pmatrix}1 & 2\\3 & 4\end{pmatrix}=\begin{pmatrix}8 & 14\\11 & 16\end{pmatrix}$$

Solution of simultaneous equations by a matrix method

A pair of simultaneous equations in two unknowns may be written as a single matrix equation:

$$2a+b=11$$
$$5a+3b=29$$

This pair of simultaneous equations in a and b may be written:

$$\begin{pmatrix}2 & 1\\5 & 3\end{pmatrix}\begin{pmatrix}a\\b\end{pmatrix}=\begin{pmatrix}11\\29\end{pmatrix}$$

The 2×2 matrix is a **matrix of coefficients**, which is then pre-multiplied by its inverse to produce the identity matrix. The equation is balanced by a pre-multiplication of the same inverse matrix on the other side of the equals sign.

$$\begin{pmatrix}3 & -1\\-1 & 2\end{pmatrix}\begin{pmatrix}2 & 1\\5 & 3\end{pmatrix}\begin{pmatrix}a\\b\end{pmatrix}=\begin{pmatrix}3 & -1\\-5 & 2\end{pmatrix}\begin{pmatrix}11\\29\end{pmatrix}$$

$$\begin{pmatrix}1 & 0\\0 & 1\end{pmatrix}\begin{pmatrix}a\\b\end{pmatrix}=\begin{pmatrix}3\times11+-1\times29\\-5\times11+ 2\times29\end{pmatrix}=\begin{pmatrix}4\\3\end{pmatrix}$$

Note here that $\triangle=1$. The solution to the equations is thus $a=4$ and $b=3$. Another example involving the determinant of the matrix of coefficients will help to explain the procedure.

Example: Solve:
$$7p-4q=12 \atop 5p-2q=9$$
This pair of simultaneous equations in p and q may be written as this single matrix equation:
$$\begin{pmatrix} 7 & -4 \\ 5 & -2 \end{pmatrix}\begin{pmatrix} p \\ q \end{pmatrix}=\begin{pmatrix} 12 \\ 9 \end{pmatrix}$$
The determinant of the matrix of coefficients is:
$$(7\times-2)-(-4\times5)=-14--20=6$$
The inverse of the matrix of coefficients is:
$$\frac{1}{6}\begin{pmatrix} -2 & 4 \\ -5 & 7 \end{pmatrix}$$
Pre-multiplying by the inverse gives:
$$\frac{1}{6}\begin{pmatrix} -2 & 4 \\ -5 & 7 \end{pmatrix}\begin{pmatrix} 7 & -4 \\ 5 & -2 \end{pmatrix}\begin{pmatrix} p \\ q \end{pmatrix}=\frac{1}{6}\begin{pmatrix} -2 & 4 \\ -5 & 7 \end{pmatrix}\begin{pmatrix} 12 \\ 9 \end{pmatrix}$$
$$\begin{pmatrix} 1 & 0 \\ 0 & 1 \end{pmatrix}\begin{pmatrix} p \\ q \end{pmatrix}=\frac{1}{6}\begin{pmatrix} 12 \\ 3 \end{pmatrix}=\begin{pmatrix} 2 \\ \frac{1}{2} \end{pmatrix}$$
Hence $p=2$ and $q=\frac{1}{2}$

Matrix equations

Using the operation rules for matrices, missing elements may be evaluated.

Examples: If:
$$\begin{pmatrix} 7n \\ 5 \end{pmatrix}-\begin{pmatrix} n \\ m \end{pmatrix}=\begin{pmatrix} 24 \\ 11 \end{pmatrix}$$
find the values for m and n.

It follows that $7n-n=24$ and $5-m=11$. This gives:
$$6n=24 \quad 5=11+m$$
$$\therefore n=4 \quad \therefore -6=m$$

Networks and matrices

1 A **network** consists of points, called **nodes**, and routes between them, called **arcs**.
2 The **order of a node** is the number of arcs which meet at that node.
3 A route which goes directly between nodes without passing through any intermediate nodes is called a **one-stage route**.

This is a single arc, such as A to B, where A and B are nodes in a network.

4 A route which passes through one intermediate node before reaching its destination is called a **two-stage route**. This is a double arc such as A to B to C, or A to B to A, where A, B and C are nodes in a network.

One-stage route matrix
The **network** of arcs between nodes may be expressed as a **one-stage route matrix**.

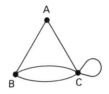

Fig. 9.1 *Network*

The network in Fig. 9.1 may be expressed as a **table of routes**:

$$
\begin{array}{c}
 & \begin{array}{ccc} To \\ A & B & C \end{array} \\
\begin{array}{c} A \\ From\ B \\ C \end{array} &
\left|\begin{array}{ccc} 0 & 1 & 1 \\ 1 & 0 & 2 \\ 1 & 2 & 2 \end{array}\right.
\end{array}
\quad \text{which becomes}\ \mathbf{R} = \begin{pmatrix} 0 & 1 & 1 \\ 1 & 0 & 2 \\ 1 & 2 & 2 \end{pmatrix}
$$

Route table   One-stage route matrix

Loops, as at C, may be traversed in each direction.
1 The one-stage route matrix $\mathbf{R}$ is always a square matrix and symmetrical along the leading diagonal (from top left to bottom right).
2 The elements in the leading diagonal are always zero or even.
3 The sum of the rows or columns gives the order of the nodes in the network.

Two-stage route matrix

The **two-stage route matrix** for a network may be found by squaring the one-stage route matrix:

$$\mathbf{R}^2 = \begin{pmatrix} 0 & 1 & 1 \\ 1 & 0 & 2 \\ 1 & 2 & 2 \end{pmatrix} \begin{pmatrix} 0 & 1 & 1 \\ 1 & 0 & 2 \\ 1 & 2 & 2 \end{pmatrix} = \begin{pmatrix} 2 & 2 & 4 \\ 2 & 5 & 5 \\ 4 & 5 & 9 \end{pmatrix}$$

Two-stage
route matrix

If N is the number of nodes, A is the number of arcs and R is the number of regions enclosed by the arcs, together with the outside region, in a given network, then:

$N + R = A + 2$ (**Euler's rule**)

Directed network

1 A **directed network** has the directions of its routes indicated by arrows.

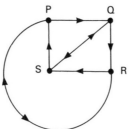

Fig. 9.2 *Directed network*

2 The directed network in Fig. 9.2 may be expressed as a table of routes:

	To			
	P	Q	R	S
P	0	1	1	0
From Q	0	0	1	1
R	1	0	0	1
S	1	1	0	0

Route table

which becomes $\begin{pmatrix} 0 & 1 & 1 & 0 \\ 0 & 0 & 1 & 1 \\ 1 & 0 & 0 & 1 \\ 1 & 1 & 0 & 0 \end{pmatrix}$

One-stage
route matrix

necessarily symmetrical about the leading diagonal.

4 Squaring the one-stage route matrix of a directed network gives the two-stage route matrix:

$$\begin{pmatrix} 0 & 1 & 1 & 0 \\ 0 & 0 & 1 & 1 \\ 1 & 0 & 0 & 1 \\ 1 & 1 & 0 & 0 \end{pmatrix}\begin{pmatrix} 0 & 1 & 1 & 0 \\ 0 & 0 & 1 & 1 \\ 1 & 0 & 0 & 1 \\ 1 & 1 & 0 & 0 \end{pmatrix} = \begin{pmatrix} 1 & 0 & 1 & 2 \\ 2 & 1 & 0 & 1 \\ 1 & 2 & 1 & 0 \\ 0 & 1 & 2 & 1 \end{pmatrix}$$

One-stage route matrix   Two-stage route matrix

5 From a route-matrix it is possible to draw the corresponding network.

Example: Draw the network for the route-matrix:

$$\begin{pmatrix} 0 & 3 \\ 3 & 2 \end{pmatrix}$$

The matrix is 2×2, so the network has two nodes, which we can call A and B. The matrix is symmetrical about the leading diagonal, so the network is not directed. There are three routes between A and B and a loop at one of the nodes. The corresponding network is shown in Fig. 9.3.

Fig. 9.3

85

10 GEOMETRY

Angle

1 **Angle** is a measurement of **turning**.
2 A whole turn is divided up into 360° (**degrees**) (Fig. 10.1(a)).
3 A half-turn of 180° makes a straight line (Fig. 10.1(b)).
4 A quarter-turn of 90° makes a square corner or **right-angle** (Fig. 10.1(c)).

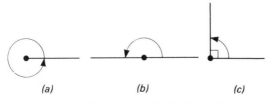

Fig. 10.1 (a) 360°; (b) 180°; (c) 90°

5 An angle between 0° and 90° is an **acute** angle.
6 An angle between 90° and 180° is an **obtuse** angle.
7 An angle between 180° and 360° is a **reflex** angle.
8 Angles which total to 90° are said to be **complementary**.
9 Angles which total to 180° are said to be **supplementary**.

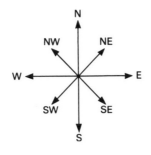

Fig. 10.2 *Compass points*

86

Bearings

1 The four main **compass points** are **north** (N), **east** (E), **south** (S) and **west** (W).
2 The compass points between them are north-east (NE), south-east (SE), south-west (SW) and north-west (NW).

3 **Bearings** are measured in degrees from north in a clockwise direction and are usually given as three figures, e.g.
   ★ east has a bearing of 090°
   ★ south has a bearing of 180°
4 The bearing of a point B from a point A gives the direction in which B lies in a straight line from A, measured clockwise from north.

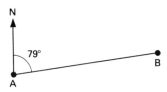

Fig. 10.3

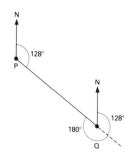

Fig. 10.4

Example: The bearing of B from A in Fig. 10.3 is 079°.

Example: The bearing of Q from P in Fig. 10.4 is 128°. The bearing of P from Q is 308° (128°+180°).

Angles and straight lines
1 **Angles on a straight line** (see Fig. 10.5) are supplementary (total to 180°).

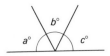

Fig. 10.5 *Angles on a straight line;* a°+b°+c°=*180°*

2 If two lines intersect, then the **vertically opposite angles** are equal (see Fig. 10.6).

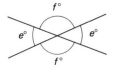

Fig. 10.6 *Vertically opposite angles*

3 Lines which are at right-angles to each other are called **perpendicular** lines.

Fig. 10.7 *Perpendicular lines*

Parallel lines

1 Lines which proceed in the same direction at a constant distance apart are called **parallel lines**, and are often indicated by arrows as shown in Fig. 10.8.

2 Lines which proceed in the same direction and whose distance apart is always zero are called **coincident lines**.

3 A line which intersects a set of parallel lines is called a **transversal**.

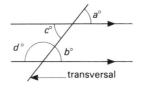

Fig. 10.9 *A transversal line*

4 Angles on the same side of the transversal and either both above or both below the parallel lines are equal. They are called **corresponding angles**. In Fig. 10.9 the angles $a°$ and $b°$ are corresponding angles.

5 Angles on opposite sides of the transversal and between the parallel lines are equal. They are called **alternate angles**. In Fig. 10.9 the angles marked $b°$ and $c°$ are alternate angles.

6 Angles on the same side of the transversal and between parallel lines are supplementary. They are called **allied angles**. In Fig. 10.9 the angles marked $c°$ and $d°$ are allied angles.

Triangles

1 A **triangle** is a three-sided shape.
2 The angle sum of a triangle is $180°$.
3 The exterior angle of a triangle is equal to the sum of the two interior opposite angles (see Fig. 10.10).

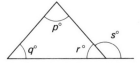

Fig. 10.10 *The angles of a triangles:* $p° + q° + r° = 180°$; $s° = p° + q°$

4 An **equilateral triangle** has three equal sides and three equal angles, each $60°$ (see Fig. 10.11).

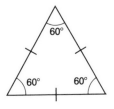

Fig. 10.11 *Equilateral triangle*

90

angles (see Fig. 10.12).

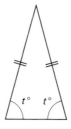

Fig. 10.12 *Isosceles triangle*

6 A **right-angled** triangle has one angle of 90°, the other two angles being complementary (see Fig. 10.13).

Fig. 10.13 *Right-angled triangle;* a° +b° =90°

7 A **scalene triangle** has three unequal sides (see Fig. 10.14).

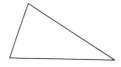

Fig. 10.14 *Scalene triangle*

Quadrilaterals

1 A **quadrilateral** is a four-sided shape.
2 A **rectangle** (see Fig. 10.15) has:
  * opposite sides that are equal and parallel;
  * all interior angles are 90°;
  * diagonals that bisect each other.

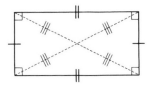

Fig. 10.15 *Rectangle*

3 A **square** (see Fig. 10.16) is a special case of a rectangle:
  * all sides are equal;
  * the diagonals are perpendicular to each other;
  * the diagonals bisect the angles.

Fig. 10.16 *Square*

4 A **parallelogram** (see Fig. 10.17) has:
  * opposite sides equal and parallel;
  * opposite angles equal, one pair being acute the other obtuse;
  * diagonals that bisect each other.

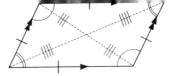

Fig. 10.17 *Parallelogram*

5 A **rhombus** (see Fig. 10.18) is a special case of a parallelogram;
   ★ all sides are equal;
   ★ diagonals are perpendicular to each other;
   ★ the diagonals bisect the angles.

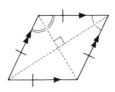

Fig. 10.18 *Rhombus*

6 A **trapezium** (see Fig. 10.19) has:
   ★ one pair of opposite sides parallel;
   ★ an isosceles trapezium has two non-parallel sides equal in length.

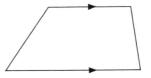

Fig. 10.19 *Trapezium*

7 A **kite** (see Fig. 10.20) has:
   * ★ adjacent pairs of sides equal;
   * ★ one pair of opposite angles equal;
   * ★ perpendicular diagonals;
   * ★ only one diagonal bisected.

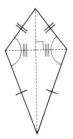

Fig. 10.20 *Kite*

8 An **arrowhead** (see Fig. 10.21) is like a kite, but has an internal reflex angle between a pair of equal sides.

Fig. 10.21 *Arrowhead*

Area properties of triangles and quadrilaterals
1 The area of a triangle is one half of the area of a parallelogram drawn on the same base and between the same parallels.

2 Parallelograms on the same base and between the same parallels are equal in area.

3 Triangles with equal bases and the same perpendicular heights have equal areas.

4 The areas of similar triangles are in the ratio of the squares on the corresponding sides.

See also Chapter 3 on area and volume

Polygons

1 A **polygon** is a many-sided plane shape with straight sides.

2 The names of some polygons:
- ★ 5 sides – pentagon
- ★ 6 sides – hexagon
- ★ 7 sides – heptagon
- ★ 8 sides – octagon
- ★ 9 sides – nonagon
- ★ 10 sides – decagon
- ★ 12 sides – dodecagon
- ★ 20 sides – icosagon

3 A **convex polygon** has only acute and obtuse internal angles.

4 A **re-entrant polygon** has at least one reflex internal angle.

5 A **regular polygon** has equal sides and equal internal angles.

6 The sum of the external angles of any convex polygon is $360°$.

7 Each external angle (see Fig. 10.22) of a regular convex n-sided polygon is $\dfrac{360°}{n}$.

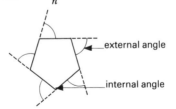

Fig. 10.22 *Polygon (a pentagon)*

8 The sum of the internal angles of a convex n-sided polygon is

$$\frac{180(n-2)°}{n} \text{ or } \left(180-\frac{360}{n}\right)°$$

Circles
1 The main parts of a **circle** are labelled in Fig. 10.23.

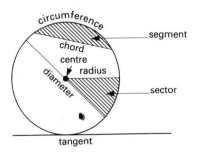

Fig. 10.23 *The main parts of a circle*

2 For any circle:
$$\frac{\text{Circumference}}{\text{Diameter}} = \pi \text{ (approx. } 3\tfrac{1}{7} \text{ or } 3.142)$$

3 For any circle of radius r, if C is its circumference and A is its area, then:
  ★ $C = 2 \times \pi \times r = 2\pi r$
  ★ $A = \pi \times r \times r = \pi r^2$
  (see Chapter 3 on area and volume)

Angle properties of a circle
The centre of a circle will be marked O in the following figures.
1 Angles at the centre of a circle are twice the size of angles at the circumference of the circle (see Fig. 10.24).

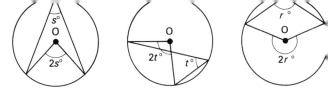

Fig. 10.24

2 Angles in a semicircle are 90° (see Fig. 10.25).

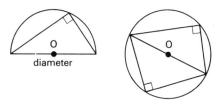

Fig. 10.25

3 Angles in the same segment are equal (see Fig. 10.26).

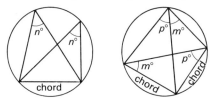

Fig. 10.26

4 Opposite angles in a cyclic quadrilateral (a four-sided shape with each corner on the circumference of the circle) are supplementary: $a° + c° = 180°$ and $b° + d° = 180°$ (see Fig. 10.27).

Fig. 10.27

Tangent properties of a circle

1 A **tangent** at any point of a circle and the radius of the circle to this point on the circumference are perpendicular (see Fig. 10.28).

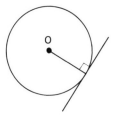

Fig. 10.28

2 The two tangents from a single point outside the circle are equal in length, and the angle between them is bisected by a line drawn from this point to the centre of the circle (see Fig. 10.29).

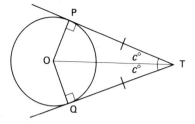

Fig. 10.29 $PT = TQ$; angle $O\hat{T}P$ = angle $O\hat{T}Q$

3 Angles between a tangent and a chord and in the **alternate segment** subtended by the chord are equal (see Fig. 10.30).

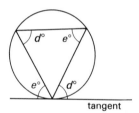

Fig. 10.30

Constructions

There are many different constructions. Consult your syllabus for requirements. Only the basic constructions are given here.

1 To construct an **angle of 60°** (see Fig. 10.31):
   ★ draw a line and mark two points A and B;
   ★ with compasses, centre A, radius AB, draw an arc above this line;

- with compasses, centre B, radius AB, draw an arc to cut the previous arc at C;
- this constructs an equilateral triangle so that angle $\hat{CAB}$ = angle $\hat{CBA}$ = angle $\hat{ACB}$ = 60°.

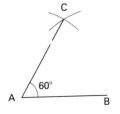

Fig. 10.31 *Constructing an angle of 60°*

2 To construct **an angle of 90°** (see Fig. 10.32):
   - draw a line and mark a point A;
   - construct a circle, centre O, passing through A;
   - name the other point of intersection between line and circle point B;
   - draw diameter of circle through B and name the other end C;
   - join AC, giving angle $\hat{CAB}$ = 90° (angle in a semicircle).

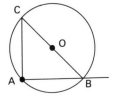

Fig. 10.32 *Constructing an angle of 90°*

3 To construct the **bisector of an angle** (see Fig. 10.33):
   - from centre A draw arcs of equal radius to cut at B and C;
   - centre B draw an arc;

* centre C draw an arc of equal radius to cut previous arc at D;
* join AD, which then bisects angle BÂC.

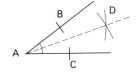

Fig. 10.33 *Bisecting an angle*

4 To construct an **angle of 30°** construct an angle of 60° and bisect it, as above.
5 To construct an **angle of 45°** construct an angle of 90° and bisect it, as above.
6 To construct the **perpendicular bisector of a line** (see Fig. 10.34):
   * centre A, radius more than $\frac{1}{2}$ AB, draw arcs above and below the line;
   * centre B, same radius, draw arcs to cut previous arcs at C and D;
   * join C and D; this line is the perpendicular bisector of AB.

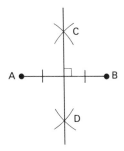

Fig. 10.34 *Constructing a perpendicular bisector of a line*

101

Locus

The **locus of a point** is the path traced out by the point which moves such that it satisfies given conditions. It may consist of a single point, some isolated points, one or more straight or curved lines, or a region of a plane or space.

1 The locus of a point which is equidistant from a fixed point is a circle with the fixed point as centre, and radius the given distance (see Fig. 10.35). (In three dimensions it is a sphere.)

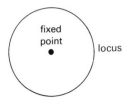

Fig. 10.35

2 The locus of a point which is equidistant from a fixed infinite line is a pair of parallel lines which are this distance either side of the line (see Fig. 10.36). (In three dimensions it is a cylinder.)

——————————————————— locus

— — — — — — — — — — — — — — line

——————————————————— locus

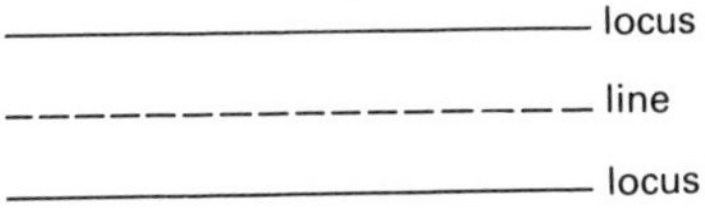

Fig. 10.36

3 The locus of a point which is equidistant from a fixed finite line is a pair of parallel lines joined by two semicircular ends (see Fig. 10.37). (In three dimensions it is a cylinder with hemispherical ends.)

102

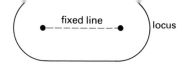

Fig. 10.37

11 TRANSFORMATIONS

Reflection

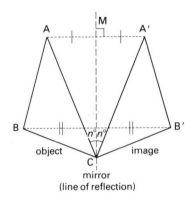

Fig. 11.1 *Reflection*

1 A **reflection** is a transformation which leaves lengths and areas unchanged
2 In Fig. 11.1 point A on the **object** is reflected in the mirror line into point A' on the **image**.
3 The line AA' is perpendicular to the mirror and meets it at point M. All lines joining points on the object to their reflected images (except for points on the mirror line) are perpendicular to the mirror line.
4 The distances AM and MA' are equal.
5 Point C on the object is also on the mirror line. The reflection leaves the position of C unchanged.
6 Angle AĈM = angle MĈA'.
7 To find a line of reflection between two congruent shapes, one being the reflection of the other, construct the perpendicular bisector between two corresponding points on the shapes.

reflection.

9 The point with coordinates (a,b) when reflected in the x axis becomes the point $(a, -b)$ (see Fig. 11.2).

10 The point with coordinates (a,b) when reflected in the y axis becomes the point $(-a,b)$.

11 The point with coordinates (a,b) when reflected in the line with equation $y=x$ becomes the point (b,a).

12 The point with coordinates (a,b) when reflected in the line with equation $y=-x$ becomes the point $(-b,-a)$.

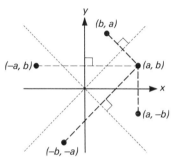

Fig. 11.2

Rotation

1 A **rotation** is a transformation which leaves lengths and areas unchanged.

2 In Fig. 11.3 point P on the **object** is rotated about the **centre of the rotation**, C, through an angle of $n°$, to point P' on the **image**.

3 Positive rotations are measured anticlockwise; negative rotations are measured clockwise.

4 A rotation of $n°$ is the same as a rotation of $-(360-n)°$ about the same centre. For example, $^+100°$ is the same as $^-260°$.

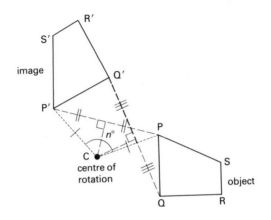

Fig. 11.3. *Rotation*

5 The lengths CP and CP' are equal, being the radius of the rotation.
6 The other points on the object are similarly rotated:
   ★ CQ=CQ' and angle QĈQ'=$n°$
   ★ CR=CR' and angle RĈR'=$n°$
   ★ CS=CS' and angle SĈS'=$n°$
7 The perpendicular bisectors of PP', QQ', RR' and SS' pass through the centre of the rotation. This is used as a technique for finding an unknown centre of rotation.
8 The point with coordinates (a,b) when rotated about the origin through $+90°$ becomes the point $(-b,a)$ (see Fig. 11.4).
9 The point with coordinates (a,b) when rotated about the origin through $+180°$ becomes the point $(-a,-b)$.
10 The point with coordinates (a,b) when rotated about the origin through $+270°$ becomes the point $(b,-a)$.

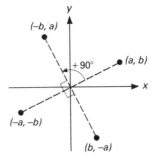

Fig. 11.4

Translation

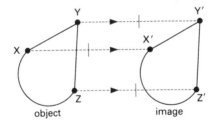

Fig. 11.5 *Translation*

1 A **translation** is a transformation which leaves lengths, directions and areas unchanged.
2 In Fig. 11.5 point X on the **object** is translated (moved) in a **fixed direction** for a **fixed distance** to point X' on the **image**.
3 All points on the object move in the same direction for the same distance:

107

* XX'=YY'=ZZ';
  * XX', YY' and ZZ' are parallel lines.
4 A translation is defined by its distance and direction. This may be given as either a length together with a bearing, or as a vector displacement; for example:
  * 6cm parallel to the x axis, or
  * $\binom{6}{0}$ (see Chapter 14 on vectors).

Shear

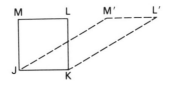

Fig. 11.6 *Shear*

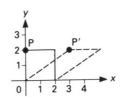

Fig. 11.7

1 A **shear** is a transformation which leaves areas unchanged.
2 In Fig. 11.6 the square JKLM is sheared into the parallelogram JKL'M'.
3 The line JK remains unchanged and is the **invariant line** of the shear. This gives the direction of the shear. All points move parallel to this line.

4 A shear is defined by stating the invariant line and giving the displacement of one point on the figure which is not on the invariant line.

Example: Shear parallel to the x axis (invariant) with point P $(0,2)$ transformed to point P' $(3,2)$ (see Fig. 11.7).

Example: Shear parallel to the x axis (invariant) with point Q $(1,3)$ transformed to point Q' $(4,3)$ (see Fig. 11.8).

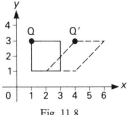

Fig. 11.8

Stretch

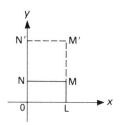

Fig. 11.9 *Stretch*

1 In Fig. 11.9 the rectangle OLMN is **stretched** into the rectangle OLM'N'.

2 The line OL remains unchanged and is the **invariant line** of the stretch. All points not on this line are transformed in a direction perpendicular to it.

3 The size of the stretch is given as a scale factor. If $LM \times n = LM'$, then n is the scale factor of this stretch.

4   The stretch scale factor may be positive or negative, integral or fractional.
5   A stretch is defined by stating the invariant line and giving the stretch scale factor.

Example:
Stretch parallel to the x axis; invariant line is the y axis; scale factor $\times 3$. Point P $(2,2)$ is transformed to point P^1 $(6,2)$ (see Fig. 11.10).

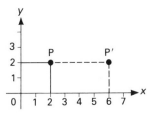

Fig. 11.10

Example:
Stretch parallel to the y axis; invariant line is the x axis; scale factor $\times 1\frac{1}{2}$. Point Q $(3,2)$ is transformed to point Q' $(3,3)$ (see Fig. 11.11).

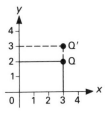

Fig. 11.11

110

Enlargement (magnification)

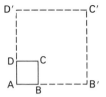

Fig. 11.12 *Enlargement*

1 An **enlargement** is an equal stretch in two perpendicular directions.
2 In Fig. 11.12 the square ABCD is **enlarged** into the square AB'C'D'.
3 The point A is unchanged and is the **centre of the enlargement**.
4 The size of the enlargement is given as a scale factor. If $AB \times n = AB'$, then n is the enlargement scale factor.
5 The enlargement scale factor may be positive or negative, integral or fractional.
6 The area change produced by an enlargement is the square of the scale factor (n^2).
7 An enlargement is defined by giving the centre of the enlargement and the enlargement scale factor.

Example: Enlargement centre P with scale factor $\times 2$ (see Fig. 11.3).

Fig. 11.13

Example: Enlargement centre Q with scale factor $\times -1\frac{1}{2}$ (see Fig. 11.14).

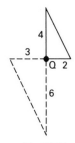

Fig. 11.14

Transformation matrices

A 2×2 **transformation matrix** transforms point $P(x, y)$ into point $P'(x', y')$ by pre-multiplication, as shown here:

$$\begin{pmatrix} a & b \\ c & d \end{pmatrix}\begin{pmatrix} x \\ y \end{pmatrix}=\begin{pmatrix} x' \\ y' \end{pmatrix}$$

If it is necessary to find an appropriate transformation matrix, consider the two points $(1,0)$ and $(0,1)$. Let the images of these two points be (x_1, y_1) and (x_2, y_2) respectively. The required transformation matrix will be:

$$\begin{pmatrix} x_1 & x_2 \\ y_1 & y_2 \end{pmatrix}$$

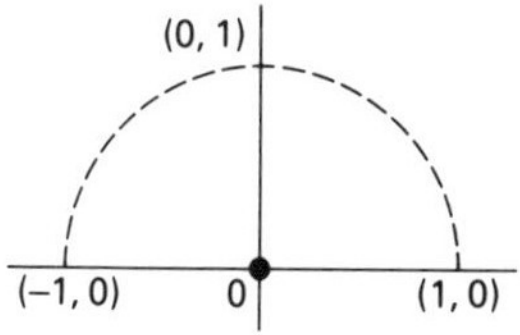

Fig. 11.15

Example: To find the 2×2 matrix for a rotation of $+90°$ about the origin (see Fig. 11.15):

$(1,0)$ goes to $(0,1)$ and
$(0,1)$ goes to $(-1,0)$

The required matrix is:

$$\begin{pmatrix} 0 & -1 \\ 1 & 0 \end{pmatrix}$$

Some standard transformation matrices

1 Reflection in x axis:
$$\begin{pmatrix} 1 & 0 \\ 0 & -1 \end{pmatrix}$$

2 Reflection in y axis:
$$\begin{pmatrix} -1 & 0 \\ 0 & 1 \end{pmatrix}$$

3 Reflection in $y=x$:
$$\begin{pmatrix} 0 & 1 \\ 1 & 0 \end{pmatrix}$$

4 Reflection in $y=-x$:
$$\begin{pmatrix} 0 & -1 \\ -1 & 0 \end{pmatrix}$$

5 Rotation $+90°$ about $(0,0)$:
$$\begin{pmatrix} 0 & -1 \\ 1 & 0 \end{pmatrix}$$

6 Rotation $+180°$ about $(0,0)$:
$$\begin{pmatrix} -1 & 0 \\ 0 & -1 \end{pmatrix}$$

7 Rotation $+270°$ about $(0,0)$:
$$\begin{pmatrix} 0 & 1 \\ -1 & 0 \end{pmatrix}$$

8 No change:
$$\begin{pmatrix} 1 & 0 \\ 0 & 1 \end{pmatrix}$$

9 Rotate $n°$ about $(0,0)$:
$$\begin{pmatrix} \cos n° & -\sin n° \\ \sin n° & \cos n° \end{pmatrix}$$

10 Shear parallel to x axis:

$$\begin{pmatrix} 1 & a \\ 0 & 1 \end{pmatrix}$$

The value of a affects the displacement.

11 Shear parallel to y axis:

$$\begin{pmatrix} 1 & 0 \\ b & 1 \end{pmatrix}$$

The value of b affects the displacement.

12 Stretch parallel to x axis, scale factor $\times c$:

$$\begin{pmatrix} c & 0 \\ 0 & 1 \end{pmatrix}$$

13 Stretch parallel to y axis, scale factor $\times d$:

$$\begin{pmatrix} 1 & 0 \\ 0 & d \end{pmatrix}$$

14 Enlargement centre $(0,0)$, scale factor $\times e$:

$$\begin{pmatrix} e & 0 \\ 0 & e \end{pmatrix}$$

15 Stretch parallel to x axis, scale factor $\times f$ and stretch parallel to y axis, scale factor $\times g$:

$$\begin{pmatrix} f & 0 \\ 0 & g \end{pmatrix}$$

Area factor $\times fg$.

Determinant of a transformation matrix

1 The determinant $\triangle$ of a transformation matrix gives the area change factor.

$$\begin{pmatrix} a & b \\ c & d \end{pmatrix} \quad \triangle = ad - bc$$

Example: The transformation matrix $\begin{pmatrix} 2 & 0 \\ 0 & 1 \end{pmatrix}$ produces an area change of $\times 2$.

2 If the determinant of the transformation matrix is negative, the transformation will incorporate a reflection.

3 If the determinant of the transformation matrix is zero, a shape will be transformed into a straight line (zero area).

4 If the determinant of the transformation matrix is one, the area of a shape remains unchanged.

Combined transformations

If two transformations are combined, the matrix of the combined transformation is the product of the matrices of the two separate transformations *in this order*:

$$\begin{pmatrix} \text{Combined} \\ \text{transformation} \\ \text{Matrix} \end{pmatrix} = \begin{pmatrix} \text{Matrix for 2nd} \\ \text{transformation} \end{pmatrix} \times \begin{pmatrix} \text{Matrix for 1st} \\ \text{transformation} \end{pmatrix}$$

Example: A reflection in the *x* axis (1st transformation) followed by a rotation of $+90°$ about the origin $(0,0)$ (2nd transformation) may be combined into a single transformation of a reflection in the line $y=x$:

$$\begin{pmatrix} 0 & -1 \\ 1 & 0 \end{pmatrix} \qquad \begin{pmatrix} 1 & 0 \\ 0 & -1 \end{pmatrix} = \qquad \begin{pmatrix} 0 & 1 \\ 1 & 0 \end{pmatrix}$$

2nd $\qquad\qquad$ 1st $\qquad\qquad$ Combined
$\begin{cases} \text{Rotate } ^+90° \\ \text{about } (0,0) \end{cases}$ $\quad \begin{cases} \text{Reflect} \\ \text{in } x \text{ axis} \end{cases}$ $\quad \begin{cases} \text{Reflect} \\ \text{in } y=x \end{cases}$

Inverse transformation

1 A transformation which transforms the points on the image back to the points on the object is an **inverse transformation**.
2 The inverse of the transformation matrix gives the matrix for the inverse transformation.

Example: If

$\mathbf{T} = \begin{pmatrix} 0 & -1 \\ 1 & 0 \end{pmatrix}$ (rotate $+90°$ about origin) then

$\mathbf{T}^{-1} = \begin{pmatrix} 0 & 1 \\ -1 & 0 \end{pmatrix}$ (rotate $+270°$ about origin).

Rotate $+270°$ about origin is the inverse transformation of rotate $+90°$ about origin.

3 If $\triangle$ of a transformation matrix is zero then there is no inverse transformation or matrix.

12 SYMMETRY (PLANE FIGURES)

Reflective symmetry

1 **Lines of reflective symmetry** are shown in Fig. 12.1 as dotted lines.

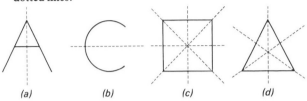

Fig. 12.1 *Lines of reflective symmetry: (a) one; (b) one; (c) four; (d) three*

2 For every point on one side of the line there is a corresponding point on the other side.
3 The distances of these corresponding points to the line of reflective symmetry are equal.
4 The lines joining these corresponding points are perpendicular to the line of reflective symmetry.
5 One half of the diagram is the mirror image of the other half (see Chapter 11 on reflections).

Rotational symmetry

1 **Centres of rotational symmetry** are shown in Fig. 12.2 as dots.

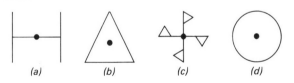

Fig. 12.2 *Orders of rotational symmetry: (a) order 2; (b) order 3; (c) order 4; (d) infinite order*

116

2 The number of times a diagram takes a position which is identical to its original position as it makes a complete turn about the centre of rotation is the **order of rotational symmetry**.

3 An irregular shape has rotational symmetry of order 1.

Point symmetry

1 The diagrams in Fig. 12.3 have **centres of point symmetry** shown as dots.

Fig. 12.3

2 A diagram which maps onto itself under an enlargement, scale factor $\times -1$, has point symmetry about the centre of the enlargement.

3 A diagram which has point symmetry also has rotational symmetry of an **even** order.

Symmetry of regular polygons

Polygon name	Number of reflective lines	Order of rotational symmetry
Equilateral triangle	3	3
Square	4	4
Pentagon	5	5
Hexagon	6	6
n-sided regular polygon	n	n

117

Symmetry of other plane figures

Name of figure	Number of reflective lines	Order of rotational symmetry
Isosceles triangle	1	1
Rectangle	2	2
Parallelogram	0	2
Rhombus	2	2
Isosceles trapezium	1	1
Kite and arrowhead	1	1
Circle	infinite (any diameter)	infinite

13 THE THEOREM OF PYTHAGORAS

The theorem

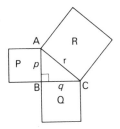

Fig. 13.1

1 In Fig. 13.1 ABC is a **right-angled triangle** in which angle $\hat{B}=90°$, $AB=p$, $BC=q$ and $AC=r$

2 Squares are drawn on each side of the triangle ABC. The areas of these squares are shown as P, Q and R.

3 It follows that:
   $P=p^2$, $Q=q^2$, $R=r^2$

4 The theorem of Pythagoras states that:
   $P+Q=R$

5 Hence:
   $p^2+q^2=r^2$

6 The sum of the squares of the two shorter sides of a right-angled triangle is equal to the square of the longest side. This holds true for all right-angled triangles.

Pythagorean triples

Some right-angled triangles with sides which are whole numbers of units are given below. The sides p and q (the shorter sides) are interchangeable; the hypotenuse (the longest side) r is always the largest value.

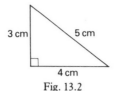

Fig. 13.2

In Fig. 13.2 it will be seen that:
$$3^2 + 4^2 = 9 + 16$$
$$= 25$$
$$= 5^2$$

p	q	r
3	4	5
5	12	13
8	15	17
7	24	25

Multiples of these Pythagorean triples give further useful triples:
6   8   10   (3   4   5 multiplied by 2)
$2\frac{1}{2}$ 6 $6\frac{1}{2}$ (5   12   13 multiplied by $\frac{1}{2}$)

Finding a missing length in a right-angled triangle

To find one of the shorter sides

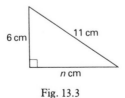

Fig. 13.3

To calculate the length of the missing side, marked as n cm in Fig. 13.3, using the theorem of Pythagoras:

$$6^2 + n^2 = 11^2$$
$$36 + n^2 = 121$$
$$n^2 = 121 - 36$$
$$n^2 = 85$$
$$n = \sqrt{85} = 9.220 \text{ cm (4 SF)}$$

To find the longest side (hypotenuse)

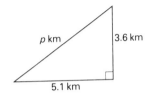

p km   3.6 km

5.1 km

Fig. 13.4

To calculate the length of the missing side, marked as p km in Fig. 13.4 using the theorem of Pythagoras:

$$p^2 = 3.6^2 + 5.1^2$$
$$p^2 = 12.96 + 26.01$$
$$p^2 = 38.97$$
$$p = \sqrt{38.97} = 6.243 \text{ km (4 SF)}$$

Problem solving

Example: One of the sides of a right-angled triangle is 14 cm longer than the shortest side but 4 cm shorter than the longest side. Find the area of the triangle.

Let the missing length be k cm. The shortest side is therefore $(k-14)$ cm and the longest side is $(k+4)$ cm (see Fig. 13.5).

121

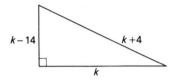

Fig. 13.5

By the theorem of Pythagoras:
$$(k-14)^2+k^2=(k+4)^2$$
$$k^2-28k+196+k^2=k^2+8k+16$$
$$k^2-36k+180=0$$
$$(k-6)(k-30)=0$$
$$k=6 \text{ or } 30$$

It will be seen that k cannot equal 6, otherwise the lengths of the triangle would have negative values. Hence the lengths of the triangle are 16 cm $(30-14)$, 30 cm and 34 cm $(30+4)$.

Area of the triangle $=\frac{1}{2}\times$ base length $\times$ height
$$=\frac{1}{2}\times30\times16$$
$$=240 \text{ cm}^2$$

14 VECTORS

Definition and notation

1 A **vector** is a **directed line segment**, i.e. a distance measured in a certain direction. The distance might represent other magnitudes such as the velocity of an object.

2 Two methods of symbolizing a vector are used:
- ★ $\overrightarrow{PQ}$ gives the endpoints P and Q of the vector with the direction indicated by the arrow;
- ★ **a** is an algebraic symbolization of a vector.

Column vectors

The distance and direction of a vector are given as a 2×1 column matrix. The elements of the matrix indicate the distance travelled horizontally to the right from the starting point, followed by the distance travelled vertically upwards to the finishing point. Negative elements are used for the directions left and down, respectively.

1 See Fig. 14.1:

$$\overrightarrow{PQ} = \begin{pmatrix} 3 \\ 4 \end{pmatrix}$$

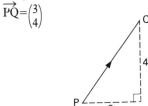

Fig. 14.1

- ★ P is the starting point and Q the finishing point.
- ★ The arrow shows the direction of the vector.

2 See Fig. 14.2:

$$\overrightarrow{AB} = \begin{pmatrix} -2 \\ 5 \end{pmatrix}$$

123

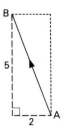

Fig. 14.2

3 In Fig. 14.2 $\overrightarrow{BA}$ would be written as $\begin{pmatrix} 2 \\ -5 \end{pmatrix}$.

4 $\overrightarrow{BA} = -\overrightarrow{AB} = -\begin{pmatrix} -2 \\ 5 \end{pmatrix} = \begin{pmatrix} 2 \\ -5 \end{pmatrix}$

5 See Fig. 14.3:

$\overrightarrow{XY} = \begin{pmatrix} -6 \\ -1 \end{pmatrix}$

Fig. 14.3

Equal vectors

1 If two vectors are equal they have the same magnitude and direction and are parallel or coincident (see Fig. 14.4).

Fig. 14.4

124

2 If $\overrightarrow{CD}=\overrightarrow{EF}$ (see Fig. 14.5) then:

  ★ CD is parallel to EF and in the same direction; and
  ★ CD=EF.

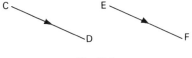

Fig. 14.5

3 If $\overrightarrow{JK}=2\overrightarrow{LM}$ (see Fig. 14.6) then:

  ★ JK is parallel to LM; and
  ★ JK=2LM.

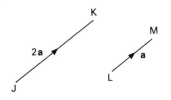

Fig. 14.6

4 If PQ is not parallel or coincident to RS then $\overrightarrow{PQ}\neq\overrightarrow{RS}$ (see Fig. 14.7).

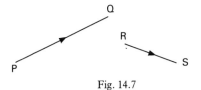

Fig. 14.7

Length of vector

We use the theorem of Pythagoras to find the length of a vector.

Example: See Fig. 14.8:

$$\overrightarrow{PQ}=\begin{pmatrix}3\\4\end{pmatrix}$$

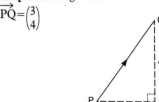

Fig. 14.8

$PQ^2=3^2+4^2=9+16=25$
$PQ=5$

Example: See Fig. 14.9:

$$\overrightarrow{RS}=\begin{pmatrix}8\\0\end{pmatrix}$$

R ————————▶———————— S
              8

Fig. 14.9

$RS=8$

Addition of vectors

Sum of vectors
The **sum of two vectors** is another vector. This result is achieved by making a triangle of vectors.

Example: If $\overrightarrow{AB}=\begin{pmatrix}6\\2\end{pmatrix}$ and $\overrightarrow{BC}=\begin{pmatrix}3\\5\end{pmatrix}$ (see Fig. 14.10), then:

$$AB+BC=\begin{pmatrix}0\\2\end{pmatrix}+\begin{pmatrix}3\\5\end{pmatrix}=\begin{pmatrix}9\\7\end{pmatrix}$$

$$=\overrightarrow{AC}$$

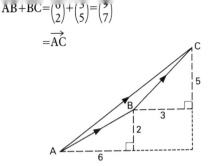

Fig. 14.10

The triangle of vectors is:

$$\overrightarrow{AB}+\overrightarrow{BC}=\overrightarrow{AC}$$

Note that point B is the link which makes it possible to add together the two vectors.

Sum of more than two vectors

1   The sum of more than two vectors is possible, the result being another vector:

$$\overrightarrow{PQ}+\overrightarrow{QR}+\overrightarrow{RS}=\overrightarrow{PS}$$

2   Notice that the vectors must be linked, otherwise the sum is not possible.

3   It is not possible to sum these vectors:

$$\overrightarrow{AB} \text{ and } \overrightarrow{CD}$$

unless we can find a vector which links them together, such as $\overrightarrow{BC}$.

Subtraction of vectors

The **difference of two vectors** is another vector. This result is achieved by making a triangle of vectors.

Example: If $\mathbf{a}=\begin{pmatrix}7\\1\end{pmatrix}$ and $\mathbf{b}=\begin{pmatrix}2\\4\end{pmatrix}$ (see Fig. 14.11) then:

$$\mathbf{a}-\mathbf{b}=\begin{pmatrix}7\\1\end{pmatrix}-\begin{pmatrix}2\\4\end{pmatrix}=\begin{pmatrix}5\\-3\end{pmatrix}$$

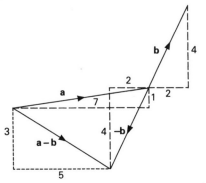

Fig. 14.11

Alternatively:

$$\mathbf{a}-\mathbf{b}=\mathbf{a}+(-\mathbf{b})=\begin{pmatrix}7\\1\end{pmatrix}+\begin{pmatrix}-2\\-4\end{pmatrix}=\begin{pmatrix}5\\-3\end{pmatrix}$$

Example:

$$\overrightarrow{CD}-\overrightarrow{ED}=\overrightarrow{CD}+(-\overrightarrow{ED})=\underbrace{\overrightarrow{CD}+\overrightarrow{DE}}=\overrightarrow{CE}$$

$$\overrightarrow{CD}=\underbrace{\overrightarrow{CE}+\overrightarrow{ED}}$$

Geometrical vectors

1 If ABCD is a square (see Fig. 14.12) then it follows that:

128

$$\overrightarrow{AB}=\overrightarrow{DC} \text{ and } \overrightarrow{AD}=\overrightarrow{BC}$$

Fig. 14.12 *Vectors in a square*

2 If JKLM is a parallelogram (see Fig. 14.13) then it follows that:

$$\overrightarrow{JK}=\overrightarrow{ML} \text{ and } \overrightarrow{JM}=\overrightarrow{KL}$$

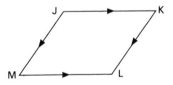

Fig. 14.13 *Vectors in a parallelogram*

3 If PQRS is a trapezium (see Fig. 14.14) then it follows that $n\overrightarrow{PQ}=\overrightarrow{SR}$, where *n* is a real number.

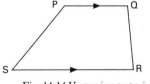

Fig. 14.14 *Vectors in a trapezium*

129

Example: WXYZ is a quadrilateral in which $\overrightarrow{WX}=2\overrightarrow{ZY}=2\mathbf{a}$, and $\overrightarrow{WZ}=\mathbf{b}$. M is the midpoint of WX. Find the following vectors in terms of $\mathbf{a}$ and $\mathbf{b}$:

1 $\overrightarrow{YZ}$; 2 $\overrightarrow{WY}$; 3 $\overrightarrow{YX}$; 4 $\overrightarrow{ZM}$; 5 $\overrightarrow{ZX}$; 6 $\overrightarrow{MY}$.

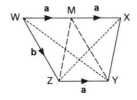

Fig. 14.15

From the information given, WX is parallel to ZY, so WXYZ is a trapezium (see Fig. 14.15). Since M is the midpoint of WX:

$\overrightarrow{WM}=\overrightarrow{MX}=\mathbf{a}$

1 $\overrightarrow{YZ}=-\overrightarrow{ZY}=-\mathbf{a}$
2 $\overrightarrow{WY}=\overrightarrow{WZ}+\overrightarrow{ZY}=\mathbf{b}+\mathbf{a}=\mathbf{a}+\mathbf{b}$
3 $\overrightarrow{YX}=\overrightarrow{YZ}+\overrightarrow{ZW}+\overrightarrow{WX}=-\mathbf{a}-\mathbf{b}+2\mathbf{a}=\mathbf{a}-\mathbf{b}$
4 $\overrightarrow{ZM}=\overrightarrow{ZW}+\overrightarrow{WM}=-\mathbf{b}+\mathbf{a}=\mathbf{a}-\mathbf{b}$

It follows that $\overrightarrow{ZM}=\overrightarrow{YX}$, so ZM is parallel to YX and both are equal in length.

5 $\overrightarrow{ZX}=\overrightarrow{ZW}+\overrightarrow{WX}=-\mathbf{b}+2\mathbf{a}=2\mathbf{a}-\mathbf{b}$
6 $\overrightarrow{MY}=\overrightarrow{MX}+\overrightarrow{XY}=\overrightarrow{MX}-\overrightarrow{YX}=\mathbf{a}-(\mathbf{a}-\mathbf{b})=\mathbf{a}-\mathbf{a}+\mathbf{b}=\mathbf{b}$, or
$\overrightarrow{MY}=\overrightarrow{MW}+\overrightarrow{WZ}+\overrightarrow{ZY}=-\mathbf{a}+\mathbf{b}+\mathbf{a}=\mathbf{b}$

It follows that $\overrightarrow{MY}=\overrightarrow{WZ}$, so MY is parallel to WZ and both are equal in length. Note that we have sufficient information to say that WMYZ and MXYZ are both parallelograms.

130

Using the properties of vectors it is possible to prove various geometrical facts.

Example: Prove that the line joining the midpoints of two adjacent sides of a triangle is parallel to, and half the length of, the third side.

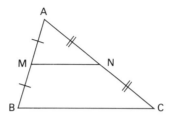

Fig. 14.16

In the triangle ABC (see Fig. 14.16) M is the midpoint of AB and N is the midpoint of AC. We need to prove that BC is parallel to MN and BC=2MN. Let $\overrightarrow{AM}=\mathbf{r}$ and $\overrightarrow{AN}=\mathbf{s}$. It follows that $\overrightarrow{MB}=\mathbf{r}$ and $\overrightarrow{AB}=2\mathbf{r}$, and that $\overrightarrow{NC}=\mathbf{s}$ and $\overrightarrow{AC}=2\mathbf{s}$.

$$\overrightarrow{BC}=\overrightarrow{BA}+\overrightarrow{AC}=-\overrightarrow{AB}+\overrightarrow{AC}=-2\mathbf{r}+2\mathbf{s}=2\mathbf{s}-2\mathbf{r}=2(\mathbf{s}-\mathbf{r})$$
$$\overrightarrow{MN}=\overrightarrow{MA}-\overrightarrow{AN}=-\overrightarrow{AM}+\overrightarrow{AN}=-\mathbf{r}+\mathbf{s}=\mathbf{s}-\mathbf{r}$$

But:

$$\overrightarrow{BC}=2(\mathbf{s}-\mathbf{r})=2\overrightarrow{MN}$$

If $\overrightarrow{BC}=2\overrightarrow{MN}$, then BC is parallel to MN and BC=2MN, so the required result is proved.

Vector equations

The following is an example of a vector equation:

$$\mathbf{a}(h-k)=\mathbf{b}(1-2h)$$

where h and k are real numbers. If it is known that the vectors **a**

131

and **b** are not parallel or coincident, then it follows that $a \neq b$, which indicates that the brackets on either side of the equation must be zero:

$h - k = 0$ and $1 - 2h = 0$

$\therefore h = \frac{1}{2}$ and $k = \frac{1}{2}$

Vector ratio

Some geometrical results may be proved by vector methods.

Example: Prove that the lines drawn from points of a triangle to the midpoints of opposite sides (medians) intersect in the ratio 2:1 (which locates the position of the centre of gravity of a plane triangle)

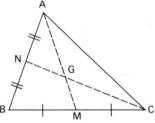

Fig. 14.17

In Fig. 14.17 M is the midpoint of BC and N is the midpoint of AB in the triangle ABC. Two medians are drawn, AM and CN, which intersect at G. It is necessary to show that AG:GM and CG:GN are both 2:1, so let $\overrightarrow{BM} = \mathbf{r}$ and $\overrightarrow{BN} = \mathbf{s}$ (so $\mathbf{r} \neq \mathbf{s}$). It follows that:

$\overrightarrow{MC} = \mathbf{r}$ and $\overrightarrow{BC} = 2\mathbf{r}$

$\overrightarrow{NA} = \mathbf{s}$ and $\overrightarrow{BA} = 2\mathbf{s}$

In triangle AMB:

$$\overrightarrow{AM}=\overrightarrow{AB}+\overrightarrow{BM}=-2s+r=r-2s$$

Let $\overrightarrow{AG}=h\overrightarrow{AM}$ where h is a real number, so:

$$\overrightarrow{AG}=h(r-2s)$$

In triangle CNB:

$$\overrightarrow{CN}=\overrightarrow{CB}+\overrightarrow{BN}=-2r+s=s-2r$$

Let $\overrightarrow{CG}=k\overrightarrow{CN}$ where k is a real number, so:

$$\overrightarrow{CG}=k(s-2r)$$

In triangle ABC:

$$\overrightarrow{AC}=\overrightarrow{AB}+\overrightarrow{BC}=-2s+2r=2r-2s$$

In triangle AGC:

$$\overrightarrow{AG}=\overrightarrow{AC}+\overrightarrow{CG}$$

From above this gives:

$$h(r-2s)=2r-2s+k(s-2r)$$

This is a vector equation and, knowing that $r\neq s$, it is possible to find the values of h and k.

Expand the brackets:

$$hr-2hs=2r-2s+ks-2kr$$

Rearrange:

$$hr-2r+2kr=2hs-2s+ks$$

Factorize:

$$r(h-2+2k)=s(2h-2+k)$$

Since $r\neq s$, the brackets are zero, giving:

$$h-2+2k=0 \qquad (1)$$
$$2h-2+k=0 \qquad (2)$$

Subtracting these two equations produces:

$$-h+k=0 \text{ or } h=k$$

Substituting $h=k$ in (1) gives:

$$-2+3k=0$$
$$3k=2$$
$$k=\tfrac{2}{3} \text{ and therefore } h=\tfrac{2}{3}$$

We let $\overrightarrow{AG}=h\overrightarrow{AM}$, so this becomes $AG=\tfrac{2}{3}AM$, which makes the ratio AG:GM=2:1. We let $\overrightarrow{CG}=k\overrightarrow{CN}$, so this becomes $CG=\tfrac{2}{3}CN$, which makes the ratio CG:GN=2:1. This proves the required result.

15 TRIGONOMETRY

The right-angled triangle
1 Fig. 15.1 shows a right-angled triangle ABC.

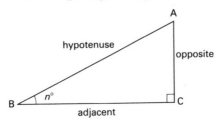

Fig. 15.1 *A right-angled triangle*

* ★ Angle $A\hat{C}B = 90°$.
* ★ Angle $A\hat{B}C = n°$.
2 The length AC is **opposite** to the angle $n°$.
3 The length BC is **adjacent** to the angle $n°$.
4 The length AB is the **hypotenuse** of the triangle (longest side, opposite the right-angle).

Sine ratio

1 In Fig. 15.1 the **sine** of angle $n° = \dfrac{AC}{AB}$

$$\sin n° = \frac{\text{Opposite length}}{\text{Hypotenuse}}$$

2 It is possible to use the sine ratio to find missing lengths in a right-angled triangle.

Example: In Fig. 15.2 we can calculate the missing length f by the sine ratio.

$$\sin 38° = \frac{\text{opp}}{\text{hyp}} = \frac{f}{12.5}$$
$$f = 12.5 \times \sin 38°$$
$$f = 7.696 \, \text{m (4 SF by calculator)}$$

134

right-angled triangle.

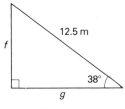

Fig. 15.2

Example: In Fig. 15.3 we can calculate the size of the missing angle $p°$ using the sine ratio.

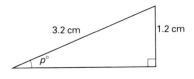

Fig. 15.3

$$\sin p° = \frac{\text{opp}}{\text{hyp}} = \frac{1.2}{3.2} = 0.375$$

$p = 22.02°$ (4 SF using the $\sin^{-1}$ key on a calculator)

Cosine ratio
1 In Fig. 15.1 the **cosine** of angle

$n° = \dfrac{\text{BC}}{\text{AB}}$

$\cos n° = \dfrac{\text{Adjacent length}}{\text{Hypotenuse}}$

135

2 It is possible to use the cosine ratio to find missing lengths in a right-angled triangle.

Example: In Fig. 15.2 we can calculate the missing length g by the cosine ratio.

$$\cos 38° = \frac{\text{adj}}{\text{hyp}} = \frac{g}{12.5}$$
$$g = 12.5 \times \cos 38°$$
$$g = 9.85 \,\text{m} \text{ (4 SF by calculator)}$$

3 It is possible to use the cosine ratio to find missing angles in a right-angled triangle.

Example: In Fig. 15.4 we can calculate the size of the missing angle $q°$ using the cosine ratio.

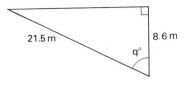

Fig. 15.4

$$\cos q° = \frac{\text{adj}}{\text{hyp}} = \frac{8.6}{21.5} = 0.4$$
$$q° = 66.42° \text{ (4 SF using the } \cos^{-1} \text{ key on a calculator)}$$

Tangent ratio

1 In Fig. 15.1 the **tangent** of angle
$$n° = \frac{\text{AC}}{\text{BC}}$$
$$\tan n° = \frac{\text{Opposite length}}{\text{Adjacent length}}$$

2 It is possible to use the tangent ratio to find missing lengths in a right-handed triangle.

Example: In Fig. 15.5 we can calculate the missing length t by the tangent ratio.

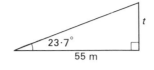

Fig. 15.5

$$\tan 23.7° = \frac{\text{opp}}{\text{adj}} = \frac{t}{55}$$
$$t = 55 \times \tan 23.7°$$
$$t = 24.14 \text{ m (4 SF by calculator)}$$

3 It is possible to use the tangent ratio to find missing angles in a right-angled triangle.

Example: In Fig. 15.6 we can calculate the size of $r°$ using the tangent ratio.

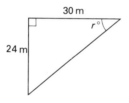

Fig. 15.6

$$\tan r° = \frac{\text{opp}}{\text{adj}} = \frac{24}{30} = 0.8$$
$$r° = 38.66° \text{ (4 SF using the } \tan^{-1} \text{ key on a calculator)}$$

Trigonometrical ratios

Taking O for the **opposite** length, A for the **adjacent** length and H for the **hypotenuse** of a right-angled triangle we get:

1   $\operatorname{Sin} n° = \dfrac{O}{H}$

2   $\operatorname{Cos} n° = \dfrac{A}{H}$

3   $\operatorname{Tan} n° = \dfrac{O}{A}$

which is often reduced to **SOHCAHTOA**.

Angle of elevation and depression

Angle of elevation
Looking up from the horizontal gives an **angle of elevation** (see Fig. 15.7).

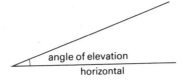

Fig. 15.7 *Elevation*

Example: The angle of elevation of a water-tower from a point 30 m from the base of the tower is 42°. Find the vertical height of the water-tower.

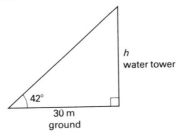

Fig. 15.8

15.8). h is the opposite length to angle $42°$ and 30 m is the adjacent length to angle $42°$, so it is necessary to use the tangent ratio (TOA):

$$\tan 42° = \frac{h}{30}$$
$$h = 30 \times \tan 42°$$
$$h = 27.01 \text{ m (4 SF by calculator)}$$

Angle of depression
Looking down from the horizontal gives an angle of depression (see Fig. 15.9).

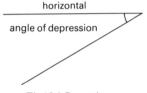

Fig 15.9 *Depression*

Example: The angle of depression of a buoy at sea from the top of a cliff 150 m high is $25°$. Find the distance from the top of the cliff directly to the buoy.

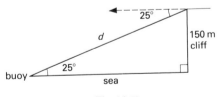

Fig. 15.10

Let the required distance be d metres (see Fig. 15.10). d is the hypotenuse of a triangle formed and 150 m is the opposite length to angle 25° (using alternate angles between the two horizontal directions), so it is necessary to use the sine ratio (SOH):

$$\sin 25° = \frac{150}{d}$$
$$d = \frac{150}{\sin 25°}$$
$$d = 354.9 \text{ metres (4 SF by calculator)}$$

Standard angles

1 Using a right-angled triangle (see Fig. 15.11) and the theorem of Pythagoras:

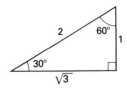

Fig. 15.11

★ $\sin 30° = \frac{1}{2}$

★ $\cos 30° = \frac{\sqrt{3}}{2}$

★ $\tan 30° = \frac{1}{\sqrt{3}}$

★ $\sin 60° = \frac{\sqrt{3}}{2}$

★ $\cos 60° = \frac{1}{2}$

★ $\tan 60° = \frac{\sqrt{3}}{1} = \sqrt{3}$

2 Using a right-angled triangle (see Fig. 15.12) and the theorem of Pythagoras:

Fig. 15.12

* $\sin 45° = \dfrac{1}{\sqrt{2}} = \cos 45°$
* $\tan 45° = \dfrac{1}{1} = 1$

3 It is also worth remembering that:
* $\sin 90° = 1$
* $\cos 90° = 0$
* $\tan 90°$ is infinite
* $\cos 0° = 1$
* $\sin 0° = 0$
* $\sin n° = \cos (90 - n)°$ if $n \leqslant 90$

Large angles

The trigonometric values for angles greater than 90° are available on many calculators. However it is worth understanding the changes in size and sign of trigonometric ratios as an angle gets larger. These are shown using the graphs of the trignometric ratios.

The sine curve

1 The curve of $y = \sin x°$ is shown in Fig. 15.13.

141

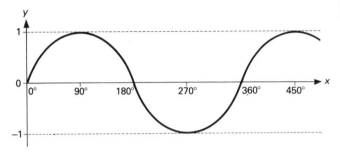

Fig. 15.13 *Sine curve;* y = *sin* x°

2 For $0° < x° < 180°$, $\sin x°$ is positive.
3 For $180° < x° < 360°$, $\sin x°$ is negative.
4 Using the symmetry of the curve, it will be seen that:
   ★ $\sin 137° = \sin 43°$ $(180° - 137°)$;
   ★ $\sin 200° = -\sin 20°$ $(200° - 180°)$.

The cosine curve
1 The curve of $y = \cos x° =$ is shown in Fig. 15.14.

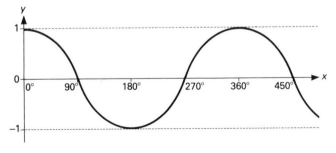

Fig. 15.14 *Cosine curve;* y = *cos* x°

142

2 For $0°<x°<90°$ and $270°<x°<360°$, cos $x°$ is positive.
3 For $90°<x°<270°$, cos $x°$ is negative.
4 Using the symmetry of the curve, it will be seen that:
   ★ $\cos 105° = -\cos 75°$ $(180°-105°)$;
   ★ $\cos 318° = \cos 42°$ $(360°-318°)$.

The tangent curve
1 The curve of $y = \tan x°$ is shown in Fig. 15.15.

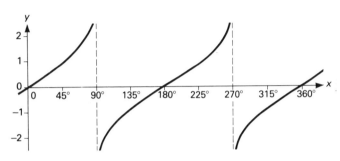

Fig. 15.15 *Tangent curve;* $y = \tan x°$

2 For $0°<x°<90°$ and $180°<x°<270°$, tan $x°$ is positive.
3 For $90°<x°<180°$ and $270°<x°<360°$, tan $x°$ is negative.
4 Note that tan $x°$ is undefined at $90°$ and $270°$.
5 Using the symmetry of the curve it will be seen that:
   ★ $\tan 156° = -\tan 24°$ $(180°-156°)$;
   ★ $\tan 212° = \tan 32°$ $(212°-180°)$.

Sine and cosine rules

The sine rule
1 In Fig. 15.16:
   $BC = a$, $AC = b$ and $AB = c$ (lengths are opposite the angles)

143

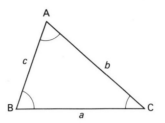

Fig. 15.16

2 For **any** triangle, the **sine rule** is:

$$\frac{a}{\sin A} = \frac{b}{\sin B} = \frac{c}{\sin C}$$

3 The **sine rule** is used when the triangle is **not** right-angled.
4 If angle A, angle B and length c are known, it is possible to find the other lengths.
   ★ Firstly find the other angle C, using the fact that the sum of the angles in any triangle is 180°.
   ★ Then use $\frac{a}{\sin A} = \frac{c}{\sin C}$ to find length a.
   ★ Then use $\frac{b}{\sin B} = \frac{c}{\sin C}$ to find length b.
5 If angle A, length a and length b are known, it is possible to find the angles and the remaining length.
   ★ Use $\frac{a}{\sin A} = \frac{b}{\sin B}$ to find angle B.
   ★ Then use the sum of the angles is 180° to find angle C.
   ★ Then use $\frac{a}{\sin A} = \frac{c}{\sin C}$ to find length c.
6 If the relevant information is not given, it may be necessary to use the cosine rule instead.

1 For **any** triangle, the **cosine rule** is:
   $$a^2 = b^2 + c^2 - (2bc \cos A) \text{ to find length } a$$
   using the symbols shown in Fig. 15.16.
2 The other versions are found by rotating the lengths a, b and c
   with the appropriate angles A, B and C:
   ⋆ $b^2 = c^2 + a^2 - (2ca \cos B)$ to find length b
   ⋆ $c^2 = a^2 + b^2 - (2ab \cos C)$ to find length c
3 Rearranging the first equation gives:
   $$\cos A = \frac{b^2 + c^2 - a^2}{2bc} \text{ to find angle A}$$
4 Similarly:
   ⋆ $\cos B = \dfrac{c^2 + a^2 - b^2}{2ca}$ to find angle B
   ⋆ $\cos C = \dfrac{a^2 + b^2 - c^2}{2ab}$ to find angle C

Three-dimensional figures

Extract a two-dimensional figure from the three-dimensional
diagram and use the trigonometrical properties given above.

Example:

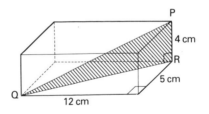

Fig. 15.17

Fig. 15.17 shows a rectangular box with dimensions
$12\,\text{cm} \times 5\,\text{cm} \times 4\,\text{cm}$. To find the angle which a diagonal from
opposite corners P and Q makes with the base, extract the
triangle PQR (see Fig. 15.18).

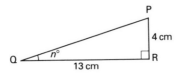

Fig. 15.18

1 Angle $\hat{R}=90°$
2 QR is the diagonal of the base and, by the theorem of Pythagoras, is 13 cm (5:12:13 triangle).
3 The required angle is $P\hat{Q}R$, which is labelled $n°$:

$$\tan n° = \frac{4}{13} = 0.3077 \text{ (4 SF)}$$

$n° = 17.1°$ (3 SF using the $\tan^{-1}$ key on the calculator)

The earth: latitude and longitude

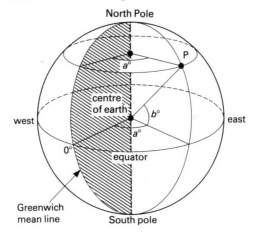

Fig. 15.19 *The earth*

146

horizontal plane of the equator).

2 Point P has **longitude** $a°$ E (measured from the vertical plane of the **Greenwich mean line** or meridian).

3 The latitude and longitude describe uniquely the position of any point on the surface of the earth.

4 A **great circle** is any circle with centre at the centre of the earth. The equator and all lines of longitude are great circles.

5 The shortest path between two points on the globe is along the circumference of a great circle.

6 A **nautical mile** is the length of an arc of a great circle which subtends an angle of one minute ($1'$; a sixtieth of a degree) at the centre of the earth.

7 A **knot** is a speed of one nautical mile per hour.

16 STATISTICS

The study of statistics involves collecting and analysing figures and data, presenting the results and making interpretations.

Data collection
1 The information is usually represented in a **frequency table**.
2 The frequency table gives the number of occurrences of each observation.

Example: Frequency table showing number of children in 30 families:

Number of children in family	Frequency
1	11
2	8
3	4
4	5
5	2
Total	30

From the table it will be seen that there were, for example, 11 families with 1 child and 5 families with 4 children.

3 The collection of data or information is called a **survey**.
4 The **range** of the distribution of family sizes given above is from one to five children.

Representing the data
1 There are two main ways of representing the data from a survey graphically so that the spread and frequency of the distribution can be seen more easily:
   ★ bar-chart or histogram;
   ★ pie-chart.
2 A **bar-chart** (see Fig. 16.1) shows the observations in columns. The height of each column depends exactly on the frequency of each observation.

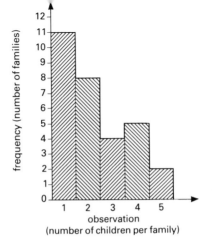

Fig. 16.1 *Family size survey; bar chart showing family size*

3   If the area of each bar is directly proportional to the frequency
    of the observations the diagram is called a **histogram**.
4   A **pie-chart** (see Fig. 16.2) shows the observations as sectors
    of a circle, the angle of each sector depending exactly on the
    frequency of each observation. In the family size survey, 360°
    divided by 30 families gives 12° for each family:

Observation (family size)	Frequency	Size of sector (in degrees)
1	11	$11 \times 12 = 132°$
2	8	$8 \times 12 = 96°$
3	4	$4 \times 12 = 48°$
4	5	$5 \times 12 = 60°$
5	2	$2 \times 12 = 24°$
Total	30	$30 \times 12 = 360°$

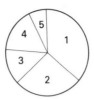

Fig. 16.2 *Pie chart showing family size.*

The mode
1 The observation with the highest frequency is called the **mode**.
2 In the family size survey, one child in the family is the modal family size. It has the highest frequency of 11 families.
3 If a survey produces two equal highest frequencies amongst the observations the distribution is said to be **bi-modal**.

The median
The observation which is in the middle of the distribution, ordered from lowest to highest value, is called the **median**.

Example:
   2, 2, 3, 5, 7, 8, 8, 8, 10
            ↑
         middle number
The median of these nine ordered numbers is 7.

There is no exact middle of an even number of observations. In the family size survey the median depends upon the 15th and 16th family from the 30 ordered family sizes. These families each have two children, so the median family size is two children. If they had been different the average of the two values would have been taken.

The mean

1   The arithmetical average of the data is called the **mean**.

2   In the family size survey the mean number of children per family is calculated as follows:

Observation (family size)	Frequency	Number of children
1	11	$1 \times 11 = 11$
2	8	$2 \times 8 = 16$
3	4	$3 \times 4 = 12$
4	5	$4 \times 5 = 20$
5	2	$5 \times 2 = \overline{10}$
		69

★ The total number of children in the survey is 69 amongst 30 families.

★ The mean number of children per family is $69 \div 30 = 1.3$

3   If the data consists of large numbers for each observation, the mean may be calculated by coding the data and working from an estimated mean.

Example: Find the mean collar-size from this data:

Collar-size	Frequency	Deviation from 16	Frequency × Deviation
14	28	-2	-56
15	122	-1	-122
16	215	0	$\overline{-178}$
17	115	1	115
18	19	2	38
	500		$\overline{153}$
			$\overline{-25}$ $(-178 + 153)$

We estimate that the mean of the 500 collar-sizes is about 16 from the spread of the distribution. We then work out the deviation from this estimated mean of 16. The *Deviation from 16* column matches with the actual collar sizes: 14 is $16 - 2$; 15 is $16 - 1$; 16 is

16−0; etc. The last column is the frequency multiplied by the deviation figure. The negative and positive deviations are summed separately, and the overall deviation of -25 is then calculated. This tells us that we have overestimated the mean.

$$\text{The actual mean} = \text{The estimated mean} \pm \frac{\text{Overall deviation}}{\text{Total frequency}}$$

$$= 16 - \frac{25}{500} = 16 - \frac{1}{20}$$

$$= 15\tfrac{19}{20}$$

Cumulative frequencies

1 If the frequencies in a frequency table are added to form a running total, the sub-totals form the **cumulative frequencies**.

2 In the family size survey the cumulative frequencies are:

Observation (family size)	Frequency	Cumulative frequency
1	11	11
2	8	19 (11+8)
3	4	23 (19+4)
4	5	28 (23+5)
5	2	30 (28+2)
Total	30	

3 The last figure in the cumulative frequency column is the total frequency.

Cumulative frequency diagram (ogive)

1 If the observations are plotted against the cumulative frequencies, the line graph produced is called the **cumulative frequency diagram** or **ogive**.

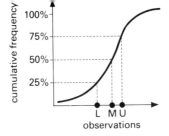

Fig. 16.3 *Ogive*

2 Fig. 16.3 shows a cumulative frequency curve. It is usually the shape of an elongated S.

3 50% of the frequency, indicated on the cumulative frequency axis, provides a reading on the observation scale, labelled M, which is the **median** of the distribution.

4 The **lower quartile** of the distribution is a value which indicates that 25% of the data lies below this value. It is labelled L in Fig. 16.4.

5 The **upper quartile** of the distribution is a value which indicates that 75% of the data lies below this value. It is labelled U in Fig. 16.4.

6 The range between the upper and lower quartile is called the **interquartile range** (U–L).

Grouped data

1 For large amounts of data the observations are often grouped into **intervals** to assist the analysis.

2 For example, in a survey of people's heights, the range may be wide. Some possible interval groupings are:

Heights in cm	Mid-interval
150–153	152
154–157	156
158–161	160
162–165	164
166–169	168
170–173	172

3 Note that a range of 150–153 in this case means any height from 150 cm up to, but not including, 154 cm.

4 In calculations of the mean the interval range is replaced by the **mid-interval** value. Note that this is the average of the lowest value of the interval with the lowest value of the next interval.

17 PROBABILITY

Definition
1 The chance of an event happening is called its **probability**.
2 A probability has a value between 0 and 1 inclusively.
3 The probability of an **impossibility** is 0
4 The probability of a **certainty** is 1

Experimental probability
It will be found by observing events that the **probability of an event** is:

$$\frac{\text{The number of times the event occurs in trials}}{\text{The total number of trials}}$$

As the number of trials increases, the experimental probability approaches the theoretical probability of an event.

Theoretical probability (or expected probability)
Out of a universal set, $\mathscr{E}$, of events, all of which are equally likely to occur, the **theoretical probability** that an event in set A occurs is written as $P(A)$.

$$P(A) = \frac{\text{Number of elements in set } A}{\text{Number of elements in } \mathscr{E}} = \frac{n(A)}{n(\mathscr{E})}$$

Example: There are 13 diamond cards in a full pack of 52 playing cards. The theoretical probability of selecting a diamond randomly from the pack is:

$$P(\text{diamond}) = \frac{13}{52} = \frac{1}{4}$$

Mutually exclusive events
An event in set A and an event in set B are said to be **mutually exclusive** if each event cannot occur at the same time. The combined probability of either event from A or event from B is given by the sum of the individual probabilities:

$$P(A \text{ or } B) = P(A) + P(B)$$

Example: There are 12 picture cards in a full pack of 52 playing cards. There are 4 aces in a pack of playing cards. If one card is selected at random, it cannot be both a picture and an ace at the same time. The events are mutually exclusive. Therefore, the probability of drawing either a picture or an ace is:

$$P \text{ (picture or ace)} = \frac{12}{52} + \frac{4}{52} = \frac{16}{52} = \frac{4}{13}$$

The combined probability of an event happening or not happening is 1.

Example: The probability of throwing a 3 or not throwing a 3 with a die is:

$$P(3 \text{ or not } 3) = \frac{1}{6} + \frac{5}{6} = \frac{6}{6} = 1$$

Non-mutually exclusive events

If an event in set A is **non-mutually exclusive** to an event in set B, then both events can occur at the same time. The combined probability of either an event from A or an event from B is given by:

$$P(A \text{ or } B) = P(A) + P(B) - P(A \cap B)$$

where $P(A \cap B)$ is the probability of the events happening at the same time.

Example: There are 12 pictures in a full pack of playing cards. There are 13 diamonds in a full pack of playing cards. There are 3 diamond pictures in a full pack of playing cards. If one card is selected at random from a full pack of playing cards, the probability that it is a picture or diamond is:

$$P \text{ (picture or diamond)} =$$
$$\underbrace{\frac{12}{52}}_{P \text{ (picture)}} + \underbrace{\frac{13}{52}}_{P \text{ (diamond)}} - \underbrace{\frac{3}{52}}_{P \text{ (picture} \cap \text{diamond)}} = \frac{22}{52} = \frac{11}{26}$$

Combined events

If two or more events occur, one after the other or together, the probabilities are combined together depending on the nature of the events.

Independent events

Independent events are such that the outcome of one event is not dependent on whether or not the other event has occurred.

The combined probability of independent events is the product of the individual probabilites:

$$P(A \text{ and } B) = P(A) \times P(B)$$

Example: A coin has one head and one tail. A die has six faces numbered 1 to 6. The outcomes of a coin being thrown and a die being cast are independent. The probability of throwing a coin and die together and getting a head and a 3 is:

$$P \text{ (head and 3)} = \frac{1}{2} \times \frac{1}{6} = \frac{1}{12}$$

Tree diagrams

Tree diagrams are useful for calculating the various probabilities which occur when a number of events happen in succession.

Example: A box contains 3 red counters and 4 blue counters. A counter is drawn at random from the box and replaced after its colour has been noted. Likewise, another counter is drawn from the box. The probabilities for the four outcomes A to D are shown in Fig. 17.1.

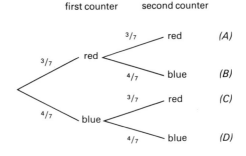

Fig. 17.1

1 (A) P (both red counters) $= \dfrac{3}{7} \times \dfrac{3}{7} = \dfrac{9}{49}$

2 (B), (C) P (one red and one blue counter) $= \dfrac{3}{7} \times \dfrac{4}{7} + \dfrac{4}{7} \times \dfrac{3}{7} = \dfrac{24}{49}$

3 (D) P (both blue counters) $= \dfrac{4}{7} \times \dfrac{4}{7} = \dfrac{16}{49}$

Conditional probability

1 If the outcome of one event is dependent on a previous event having occurred, then the combined probability of the two events is **conditional**.

2 **Conditional probabilities** occur when selections are made **without replacement** in random sampling situations.

Example: There are 13 diamonds in a full pack of playing cards. If two cards are selected, without replacement, then Fig. 17.2 illustrates the conditional probabilities of selecting or not selecting diamond cards. Note: after the first card has been selected, only 51 cards remain.

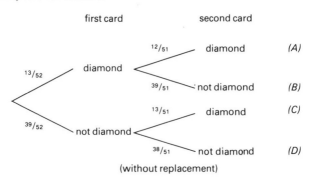

(without replacement)

Fig. 17.2

158

★ (A) P (both diamonds) $= \dfrac{13}{52} \times \dfrac{12}{51} = \dfrac{1}{4} \times \dfrac{4}{17} = \dfrac{1}{17}$

★ $(B), (C)$ P (one diamond only) $= \dfrac{13}{52} \times \dfrac{39}{51} + \dfrac{39}{52} \times \dfrac{13}{51} = \dfrac{13}{34}$

★ (D) P (no diamond card) $= \dfrac{39}{52} \times \dfrac{38}{51} = \dfrac{3}{4} \times \dfrac{38}{51}$

$$= \dfrac{1}{2} \times \dfrac{19}{17} = \dfrac{19}{34}$$

3 Note that the sum of probabilities should always be 1, since a tree diagram shows every possible outcome, i.e. in this case:

$$\dfrac{1}{17} + \dfrac{13}{34} + \dfrac{19}{34} = \dfrac{34}{34} = 1$$

18 CALCULUS

Rates of change

1 The **rate of change** of two measurements with respect to each other is called a **derivative**.

2 The rate of change of area A with respect to time t may be symbolized as:

$$\frac{dA}{dt}$$

3 The rate of change of y with respect to x on the Cartesian plane of a graph is called a **gradient**.

$$\frac{dy}{dx} = \text{gradient} = \frac{\text{Vertical displacement}}{\text{Horizontal displacement}}$$

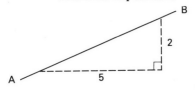

Fig. 18.1

4 The gradient of the line AB in Fig. 18.1 is $\frac{2}{5}$ or 2 in 5.

Differentiation

The process of finding the derivative $\frac{dy}{dx}$ is called **differentiation**.

If $y = ax^n$, where n is any real number, and a is a constant, then:

$$\frac{dy}{dx} = anx^{n-1}$$

Example: Find the gradient of the line with equation $y = 4x^1 - 3$ (see Fig. 18.2).

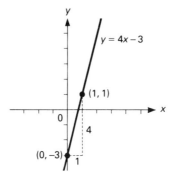

Fig. 18.2

The gradient is:
$$\frac{dy}{dx} = 4x^0 = 4$$
which is constant for a line.

Differentiation and the gradient of a curve

The **gradient of a curve** such as a parabola is not constant – it depends upon a particular point on the curve. The gradient at any point may be found by differentiation.

Example: Find the gradient of the parabola with equation $y = x^2 - 4x$ at the points $(0,0)$, $(2,-4)$ and $(4,0)$.

The gradient at any point on the curve (x,y) may be found by differentiation:
$$\frac{dy}{dx} = 2x - 4$$
Substituting the x value of a point into this formula gives the gradient at that point (see Fig. 18.3).

1 The gradient at $(0,0)$ is $2 \times 0 - 4 = -4$
2 The gradient at $(2,-4)$ is $2 \times 2 - 4 = 0$

3 The gradient at $(4,0)$ is $4 \times 2 - 4 = 4$

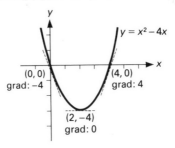

Fig. 18.3

Differentiation and the motion of objects
Differentiation may be used to solve problems concerned with the **motion of objects**.

Example: The height, s, above the ground of a stone when thrown into the air after time, t, is given by the equation:
$$s = 15t - 5t^2$$
Find the velocity of the stone when $t = 1$.

The velocity of the stone is the rate of change of height with respect to time.

$$\text{Velocity} = \frac{ds}{dt} = 15 - 10t$$

At $t = 1$ velocity is $15 - 10 \times 1 = 5$.

Maxima and minima
1 **Maximum** and **minimum** points of a curve are called its **turning points**.
2 The gradient of a curve at its maximum or minimum is zero.
3 To find a maximum or minimum value, differentiate the curve with respect to x and put $\frac{dy}{dx} = 0$.

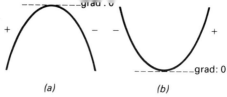

Fig. 18.4 *(a) Maximum; (b) minimum*

4 A maximum occurs when the gradient is **decreasing** with respect to x (changing from positive to negative; see Fig. 18.4 (*a*)).

5 A minimum occurs when the gradient is **increasing** with respect to x (changing from negative to positive; see Fig. 18.4 (*b*)).

6 The rate of change of the gradient is called the **second derivative**, which is symbolized by:

$$\frac{d^2y}{dx^2}$$

7 If $\frac{d^2y}{dx^2}$ is negative, a point with zero gradient is a maximum.

8 If $\frac{d^2y}{dx^2}$ is positive, a point with zero gradient is a minimum.

Example: Find the turning point of the curve $y=6x-x^2$ and determine whether it is a maximum or a minimum.

The turning point is found by differentiation:

$$\frac{dy}{dx}=6-2x=\text{gradient of the curve}$$

The gradient is zero at the turning point:

$$6-2x=0$$
$$6=2x$$
$$\therefore x=3$$

It follows from the equation of the curve that $y=9$. The turning point is (3,9). The second derivative gives:

163

$$\frac{d^2y}{dx^2} = -2$$

which is a constant negative value, hence the turning point is a maximum.

Integration
1 **Integration** is the reverse process of differentiation.
2 If:

$$\frac{dy}{dx} = ax^m$$

where m is any real number except -1 and a is a constant, then:

$$y = \frac{ax^{m+1}}{m+1} + c$$

where the value of c is a constant due to the integration.
3 This integral may be symbolized by:
$\int ax^m . dx$

Indefinite integrals
1 **Indefinite integrals** always contain the constant due to the integration because when a constant is differentiated it becomes zero.
2 The method is to increase the power of x by 1, divide by the new power and then add the constant due to the integration.

Example:
$\int (6x+1)dx = 3x^2 + x + c$

Example:
$\int (3x^2 - 4x + 5)dx = x^3 - 2x^2 + 5x + c$

Definite integrals
1 If a curve is integrated between fixed limits, the constant due to the integration is eliminated in the process of the calculation.
2 The numerical result produced represents the area between the curve, the x axis and the vertical lines given by the limits.

xample: Find the definite integral:

$$\int_0^4 (6x-x^2)dx$$

This integral represents the area which is shown as a shaded region in Fig. 18.5 between $x=0$ and $x=4$.

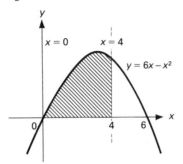

Fig. 18.5

The calculation is set out as follows:

$$\int_0^4 (6x-x^2)dx = \left[3x^2-\frac{x^3}{3}\right]_0^4$$

$$= \left(3\times4^2-\frac{4^3}{3}\right)-\left(3\times0^2-\frac{0^3}{3}\right)$$

$$= \left(48-\frac{64}{3}\right)-0$$

$$= 48-21\tfrac{1}{3}=26\tfrac{2}{3}$$

The area of the shaded region in Fig. 18.5 is $26\tfrac{2}{3}$ square units.

3 Areas under the x axis are negative when calculated by integration methods.

Notes

Notes